FINDING GOD
IN THE STORY OF
AMAZING GRACE

FINDING GOD
IN THE STORY OF
AMAZING GRACE

KURT BRUNER
JIM WARE

AN IMPRINT OF TYNDALE HOUSE PUBLISHERS, INC.

Visit Tyndale's exciting Web site at www.tyndale.com

TYNDALE is a registered trademark of Tyndale House Publishers, Inc.

SaltRiver and the SaltRiver logo are registered trademarks of Tyndale House Publishers, Inc.

Finding God in the Story of Amazing Grace

Designed by Jessie McGrath

Library of Congress Cataloging-in-Publication Data

Bruner, Kurt D.
  Finding God in the story of amazing grace / Kurt Bruner and Jim Ware.
    p. cm.
Includes bibliographical references.
  ISBN-13: 978-1-4143-1181-4 (hc)
  ISBN-10: 1-4143-1181-8 (hc)
  1. Newton, John, 1725-1807. 2. Wilberforce, William, 1759-1833.
3. Christian converts—Biography. 4. Conversion—Christianity—Biography. 5. Grace (Theology) 6. Amazing grace (Hymn) I. Ware, Jim.
II. Title.

BX5199.N55B78 2007
283.092'2—dc22   2006024299

Printed in the United States of America

11 10 09 08 07
7 6 5 4 3

Table of C*ontents*

Introduction

I'll never forget the worn, deep blue hymnals that stood symmetrically in our traditional Baptist church pew racks when I was a boy. Before I reached puberty I had spent hundreds of hours eyeing and using that sacred relic. When I was five years old, the hymnal served as an ideal table for drawing stick figures during our evangelistic preacher's poetic sermons, keeping me occupied so the grown-ups could absorb the undisturbed conviction and instruction of God's Word. By eight, I could read well enough to follow along.

Our Sunday services, while fiercely nonliturgical, still followed an equally predictable rhythm. So by the time I entered my teen years, I could recall an impressive range of lyrics from memory, enabling me to sing all four verses of the most popular hymns without glancing down at a single page. None was more familiar than "Amazing grace, how sweet the sound that saved a wretch like me. I once was lost, but now am found. Was blind, but now I see."

Like I did with most hymns, I sang along without giving the person behind these lyrics much thought. I recall noticing the name John Newton next to the title atop the page, followed by the dates 1725–1807 indicating his birth and death. But I assumed him a stoic hymn writer from two centuries past with little influence beyond our Sunday morning routine. It never occurred to me that the man who penned such famous words had been one of the more influential figures in the history of Christian faith and human rights. Nor did I have any idea how an archaic church hymn I sang from memory would connect to another, seemingly unrelated adolescent experience.

In 1977, I stumbled upon an episode of a television show I hadn't planned to watch. At fourteen years old, I was probably hoping to tune in *The Six Million Dollar Man* or some other action favorite. Instead, I found myself entranced by what would become one of the most popular series in television history. *Roots*, based upon the book by Alex Haley, depicted the story of Kunta Kinte, a young African taken from his home and forced into slavery. I had learned about such things from school textbooks. I even knew that British and American ships loaded their hulls with men, women, and children to carry them across the ocean and sell them into servitude. But I had no conception of just how awful the experience was for its victims. *Roots* opened my eyes and angered my spirit.

I watched the formerly happy, playful Kinte caged like an animal. I remember scenes from the hull where he and others were packed side by side in unspeakable conditions, lying in their own filth day after horrific day. I will never forget one

crew member trying to assuage the guilt feelings of his captain—a man who had never before carried human
"cargo"—by saying it was better for heathen Africans to live
in a "Christian" nation, even if they must be dragged off as
slaves for the privilege. My stomach tightened and turned as
I wondered who could possibly use such a flimsy argument
to justify obvious evil. Many years later I would discover that
John Newton, the same man who had penned one of my
memorized hymns, ranked among those using such justifica-
tion. In fact, John Newton had made his living as the captain
of a British slave ship.

How could a man who participated in the capture and sale
of fellow human beings—a man who transported men,
women, and children in such awful conditions that many
died en route—end up two centuries later listed in my blue
hymnal as a celebrated Christian writer? Shouldn't his sins
against humanity have disqualified him from such recogni-
tion? What is the story behind such a remarkable dichot-
omy? Much of this book is dedicated to that story, and the
God of amazing grace it reveals.

But we'll also explore another story, one that may not have
occurred without Newton's direct influence: the story of a
man named William Wilberforce.

Wilberforce, born thirty-four years after Newton, was
the politician who led a twenty-year battle in Parliament to

outlaw the British slave trade. Now the subject of a power-ful feature film, Wilberforce's story ranks among the most fascinating examples of God's intervention in the lives of ordinary, flawed people to accomplish His great work of human redemption. And, as we will discover, part of that great work includes a touching relationship between two eighteenth-century men—one a former slave-ship captain and the other, an influential British politician.

* * * * *

Redemption. What a beautiful word! The lost regained. The ruined restored. The sick healed. The broken repaired. The enslaved set free. It is a concept at the heart of Christian religion. God did not passively wait for us to get our act to-gether after the Fall. Refusing to leave sinful, hurting human-ity to wallow in its misery, He took the initiative, providing a means of redemption for His lost children and restoration for a damaged world.

Eighteenth-century Britain, the world into which Newton and Wilberforce were born, desperately needed the Al-mighty's intervention. A spiritual apathy and intellectually eviscerated religion had overtaken the church, leading many to abandon belief in God's direct involvement in human affairs. Sure, they still believed He had created the world and established certain guidelines. But only the "uneducated rabble" seemed to take such unsophisticated notions as personal sin, repentance, and salvation seriously. As a result, the church's influence as a preserving salt diminished—leaving the poor and enslaved to suffer at the hands of uncaring, wicked men.

Into such a world an emerging movement now called "evangelicalism" was born. It began in the early 1730s on the campus of Lincoln College in Oxford when four young men began meeting together weekly to read the Greek New Testament and discuss the beliefs and practices of the early church. The movement—led by John and Charles Wesley—attracted the attention and loyalty of believers hoping to recover a religion that could inspire more than social pretense and Sunday yawns. The Wesleys, George Whitefield, and others gave birth to what has been called "The Great Awakening"—a revival of sincere belief and spiritual passion in England and America that prompted men and women from all walks of life to take the tenets of Christianity seriously, and as a result, to revolutionize their world.

Both John Newton and William Wilberforce embraced a particularly evangelical Christianity. Each experienced a radical conversion—one from the profane life of a slave-ship captain, the other from the skeptical arrogance of a wealthy sophisticate. Each believed in personal sin and repentance. And each considered God's intervention in his life to include purposes beyond personal salvation. It included the call to play some part in extending God's amazing grace to others in need of redemption.

As with earlier titles in our Finding God series, this book derives inspiration from specific scenes of a great story. Previously, we discovered the theology of writers like J. R. R. Tolkien and C. S. Lewis bubbling up through their wonderful fantasy literature. In this edition, we explore how the real-life drama and writings of two great men provide insights for our own spiritual journeys. Just as the happenings of Middle-earth and Narnia reveal something of their creators, scenes from the lives of Newton and Wilberforce tell us something about the Author of history, and how His providential pen scripted scenes more intriguing than the most spectacular fiction.

We hope this book will not replace the experience of reading the actual writings or full biographies of Newton and Wilberforce. We simply wish to enhance appreciation and application of the truths that defined their influence. Each chapter opens by re-creating a scene that touches some aspect of God's intervention in and beyond their lives. While this exercise required some imaginative speculation, every chapter is inspired and informed by actual events from the lives and influence of John Newton and/or William Wilberforce.

INTRODUCTION

✻   ✻   ✻   ✻   ✻

It has been nearly three decades since I sat in my small Baptist church and held that old blue hymnal. My new liturgy includes a modern projection system and simple choruses too easily remembered. But one old hymn has survived the ever-changing litany of church worship music. We continue singing it as a deeply embedded part of the evangelical ethos—a movement that invaded apathetic churches when they needed to move beyond personal comfort and reputation to rescue the victims of an unjust world. That song continues to remind us that God does indeed intervene in human affairs, redeeming the lost and rescuing the outcast. It is a song that, like the lives of Newton and Wilberforce, points us toward a God of Amazing Grace.

PART I

John Newton

*O Lord, truly I am Your servant;
I am Your servant, the son of
Your maidservant; You have
loosed my bonds.*

PSALM 116:16

MATERNAL GRACE

Little John Newton, six years old, hoisted himself up in his chair, leaned across the table, and stared out the parlor window at the sunlight dancing on the surface of the Thames. Away flew his thoughts, beyond the river and the estuary, over the wide world, to the dim and distant figure of his father, a stern-faced man in a merchant-captain's coat, cresting the blue Mediterranean swells at the wheel of his ship.

"What are God's works of providence?"

John turned at the sound of his mother's voice, gentle but

insistent at his side. A dog-eared copy of *The Westminster Shorter Catechism* lay open in her lap.

"What are God's works of providence?" she repeated, glancing up at him.

The boy brushed the hair from his eyes. Then he blinked, rubbed his nose, and grinned. She gave him an encouraging nod.

"God's works of providence," he ventured, brightening beneath her smile, "are His most holy, wise, and powerful preserving and governing of all His creatures, and all their actions."

"Good!" she beamed. "And what special act of providence did God exercise towards man in the estate wherein he was created?"

John bit his lip and frowned. "I'm sorry, Mother," he said, his father's grim and serious face flashing before his mind's eye. "I guess I haven't learned that one yet."

"No matter," she said, hooking a finger under his chin and lifting his face up to her own. "You shall learn it tomorrow! But can you remember the song we sang together yesterday?"

"Oh, yes!" he said, clapping his hands. "Let's sing it again!"

She lifted him into her lap, and the fresh, clean smell of her white linen apron and blue taffeta skirts filled his nostrils. He snuggled close to her and they began:

Let children hear the mighty deeds which God performed of old;

4

JOHN NEWTON:
Maternal Grace

Which in our younger years we saw, and which our fathers told.

"Another!" he shouted when they had finished. "Can we sing another?"

"Why not?" she said, taking another book from the table—*The Hymns and Psalms of the Reverend Isaac Watts*. "Can you read this?" she asked, holding it up in front of him.

"O God," he said, squinting at the page, "our Help in ages past, our Hope for years to come, Our Shelter from the stormy blast, and our eternal Home."

From somewhere on the street below came the laughter and shouts of neighborhood children. They were loud and exuberant at their play, but John never heard their calls. He was too full of the scent of his mother, too enraptured with the words of the song as it rose and fell on the gentle waves of her voice.

He was in his own personal heaven.

* * * * *

"If the foundations are destroyed," says David in the eleventh Psalm, "what can the righteous do?" (Psalm 11:3). It's a question well worth pondering.

But suppose the foundations are *not* destroyed. Suppose that, on the contrary, they are laid deep in the hidden bedrock of the unchanging grace of God. Suppose that they are so well established and so painstakingly constructed that they stand unshaken despite the ravages of time and tide and chance. What then?

In that case, the righteous can hope to do *all things* (Philippians 4:13). In that case, we can expect the blind to see, the lame to walk, and the dead to live again. Best of all, we can look forward to the happy spectacle of prodigals coming home to the house built firm upon the Rock.

The story of the Reverend John Newton is the story of a beloved son, errant blasphemer, slave of slaves, and preacher of the everlasting gospel. It's a story that ends well because it *begins* well—in spite of a bleak and disastrous "middle passage."

We don't want to miss that good beginning. It's absolutely essential to everything that follows. Because for all its subsequent sordidness and sorrow, our narrative starts with a tender, touching scene: a child on his mother's knee, singing hymns and reciting verses from the Bible. An unlikely point of departure, perhaps, for a foul-mouthed sailor and a dealer in human flesh.

Elizabeth Newton, by her son's own account, was "a pious experienced Christian"[1]—a woman whose life was built around a solid vertical core. She was a genuine believer whose *knowledge* of God went deeper than mere doctrinal orthodoxy and whose *experience* of the Savior's love was warm and immediate and inextricably interwoven with the details of everyday existence.

JOHN NEWTON:
Maternal Grace

That in itself simply *had* to rub off on young John. No doubt it would have even if his mother had never said a word to him about it. There is, after all, a great deal of truth in the old maxim that faith is more effectively *caught* than *taught*. But Mrs. Newton wasn't the kind to be content with such assurances. No; she personally directed every aspect of her son's education. She saw to it that the seeds of God's righteousness, truth, and mercy were planted deep in the soil of his soul from the earliest moments of childhood.

And so, almost from the time her son could speak, Mrs. Newton began to teach him. She took his training firmly in hand with enthusiasm, devotion, and fervent prayer. The results were impressive. At three her boy was already learning to read. By four he had practically mastered the skill. At five he was memorizing Scripture, enduring the rigors of the Catechism, and filling his mind with the words and melodies of the hymns of Isaac Watts. By six he was ready to embark on the study of Latin. And all because of the industry and care of a loving mother whose heart's desire was that her son might someday serve the Lord as a minister of the Word.

But then tragedy struck. Elizabeth died before John turned seven, the victim of her own weak constitution and the ravages of consumption (or tuberculosis), one of the deadliest and most feared maladies of the day. As a result, by the time John was twenty-one, his closest companions would have been hard pressed to detect even the slightest traces of his mother's influence upon him. Among other things, anger at God over her death drove him to abandon the path she had taught him to tread. But that, as we shall see, wasn't to be the end of the story.

Though in young manhood, Newton did his level best to "sin away" every last vestige of these early impressions, he never fully succeeded. "They returned again and again," he tells us, "and it was very long before I could wholly shake them off; and when the Lord at length opened my eyes, I found a great benefit from the recollection of them."[2] In other words, Mrs. Newton's chickens eventually came home to roost.

The well-worn and oft-quoted words of Proverbs 22:6 immediately come to mind: "Train up a child in the way he should go, and when he is old, he will not depart from it." It is true, of course, that many godly parents have suffered greatly because of their wayward sons' and daughters' ill choices. As wise as this saying may be, it doesn't necessarily mean it's an unqualified promise or absolute guarantee. But neither should the life-giving principle it conveys be too easily dismissed. It does, after all, make a very real difference *how* a child is raised. Moses acknowledged this in his instructions to the people of Israel:

And these words which I command you today shall be in your heart. You shall teach them diligently to your children, and shall talk of them

JOHN NEWTON:
Maternal Grace

*when you sit in your house, when you walk by the way, when you lie
down, and when you rise up.* Deuteronomy 6:6-7

It needs to be said that, allowing for anomalies and departures from the rule, this kind of investment *generally* yields a rich dividend, a dividend that can manifest itself in surprising ways. Consider the case of young Samuel, whose course in life was fixed when his mother Hannah "lent him to the Lord" (I Samuel 1:28); or Timothy, whose "genuine faith . . . dwelt first in [his] grandmother Lois and [his] mother Eunice" (2 Timothy I:5). We know that God can use *anyone* or *anything* to draw hearts to Himself and prepare a pathway for His people. And yet there is no substitute for the tender affections of a godly mother. Newton himself felt this keenly: "[My father] was a man of remarkable good sense, and great knowledge of the world; he took great care of my morals, but could not supply my mother's part."[3]

"In the Torah," observes Chaya Saskonin, a member of Brooklyn's Lubavitch Jewish Community, "women are called *akeret ha-bayit*, the foundation of the home. That doesn't mean washing dishes. It means educating our children in everything we think about life. That's the nature of what a mother is."[4]

And so it is. It's also the nature of the God who made mothers; the God who weaves each one of us together in the womb (Psalm 139:13) and shelters us under His wings like a

9

brooding hen (Psalm 17:8; Matthew 23:37). This is the same God who, in His infinite wisdom and mercy, both gives and takes away: the God who granted John Newton an excellent parent for his early spiritual upbringing, only to remove her from his life at an unexpected hour. It seemed a cruel blow. But the upshot was that John, in the fullness of time, became "an unusual proof of His patience, providence, and grace."[5]

No wonder they call that grace "amazing."

MATERNAL GRACE
In the beginning, there is grace.

WARNING GRACE

It was a balmy Italian night: clear, moonless, and still. The midnight stars and the lights of Venice rippled brightly in the black depths of the canal. Through bleary eyes, seventeen-year-old John Newton watched the shimmering patterns converge and break and skip over the water as the jolly boat scraped up against the side of the ship.

"Look lively, lad!" laughed one of the men on deck as John's shipmates heaved him up the ladder and over the rail. "Enjoyed your time ashore a bit too much, eh?"

They trundled him below and left him swinging in his

hammock, his head spinning like a top. No sooner had he shut his eyes than the image of Mary Catlett rose before him. For the hundredth time John promised himself that, for Mary's sake, he *would not* be a crude and debauched sailor. Covering his head with one arm, he pressed his face to the canvas and slipped into darkness, seeking visions of his beloved in sleep. But it was not of Mary that he dreamed that night.

Blue stars emerged out of the darkness and winked in the rigging. He was pacing the deck in the sharp sea air, taking his turn on watch. Suddenly a figure stood before him, leaning against the rail in the shadows—how, or from where, he could not tell.

"Take this ring," said the stranger, extending his hand. On the open palm lay a circle of bright gold. "Guard it as if it were your life. While it stays safe, expect prosperity and blessing. If it is lost, abandon all hope." John took the ring and slipped it on his finger, a glow of satisfaction warming his heart. But when he glanced up to thank his benefactor, the man had vanished. *How fortunate,* thought John, *that such a talisman should fall to my keeping!*

"Or perhaps *not* so fortunate," came a second voice.

Young Newton spun on his heel only to find another dark shape standing at his side. "What do you mean?" he faltered.

The visitor sniffed. "What's the use of a worthless trinket like *that*?" he said. "If I were you, I'd waste no time losing the thing. Drop it over the side. Quick."

John blinked and stared, as if under a spell. Somehow, these strange, unwarranted words appealed to something deep inside him. Slowly, numbly, he drew the ring from his finger and flung it overboard.

Immediately the mountains above the city burst into flame. Sulfur, smoke, and the stench of death filled the air. He turned in alarm to seek an explanation, but there was no one there, only an echo of mocking laughter hanging on the air.

"Tricked!" cried John in anger and despair. "Wretched fool that I am!" But in the next instant there was a splash off the bow; and presently the first dark figure—the one who had given him the ring at first—rose out of the water, bearing the golden treasure in his hand. The fire on the mountains was snuffed in an instant. Again the night was dark and still.

"My sincere thanks!" said John, extending his hand as the shadowy shape climbed aboard. But the man shook his head and thrust his fist behind his back.

"Obviously you cannot be trusted with something so precious," said the ring-bearer. "Henceforth *I* will keep it for you."

The figure faded. The stars sputtered out. Blackness swallowed the scene.

Waking in a cold sweat, John tumbled from his hammock to the floor.

* * * * *

For John Newton, life was a miracle of grace from beginning to end. And one of the most miraculous things about it was the way God *spoke* to him at every stage, surrounding him with assurances of His love and care, hedging him about with words of admonition and exhortation, whispering cautionary messages in his ear—even when Newton wasn't particularly inclined to listen.

Young and in love, Newton had fallen for Mary Catlett, daughter of his late mother's closest friends, in December 1742. He passed up a plum of a job in Jamaica in order to maintain his home base in England—Newton sailed away at seventeen on a merchantman bound for the Mediterranean. It wasn't his first experience as a sailor: under his father's tutelage and guidance, he had taken up the life of a seafaring man at the tender age of eleven, and his moral and spiritual condition had been deteriorating ever since.

The situation seemed to have reached a low point during this journey, which took him to the Italian city of Venice. For Mary's sake, John had resolved time and time again to change his ways and improve his character. But bad company corrupts good morals, and young Newton was no exception to the rule.

"In this voyage," he confessed, "I was exposed to the company and ill example of the common sailors among whom I ranked. Importunity and opportunity presenting every day, I once more began to relax from the sobriety and order which I had observed, in some degree, for more than two years. . . . I did not, indeed, as yet turn out profligate; but I was making large strides towards a total apostasy from God."[1]

It was at this point that the voice of God broke through. While anchored in the harbor of Venice, Newton received one of the most memorable and affecting divine communications ever granted to him. It came to him through *the dream of the ring*. So overwhelming and disturbing was the impact of this message that he found himself unable to eat or sleep for several days afterward. Eventually he came to regard the vision as a kind of "last warning"—a symbolic representation of the direction his life was taking and a solemn indication of the risk he ran in despising the treasure entrusted to him in early childhood.

But though the warning left young Newton trembling, it wasn't enough to turn him around—not yet, at any rate. "The impression soon wore off," he writes, "and in a little time I totally forgot it."[2] Soon he was back in the old groove, spiraling merrily down the pathway to perdition with his rowdy shipmates. Years would pass before the dream of the ring came home to him again in a decisive, life-altering way. But when it did, he would recall its imagery with a sense of wonder. He would marvel at the miracle of *warning* grace that had been granted to him even while in a state of stubborn, self-willed rebellion.

It's a dramatic and colorful episode, unique in its particulars and picturesque in its setting. It also embodies a universal principle: However blind and stiff-necked we may be, however determined to shut our eyes against the light of the Son of Love, our heavenly Father never leaves us entirely in the dark. He shines His light into the hidden corners of our hearts and reveals to us the desperate nature of our condition. His grace goes before us every step of the way, planting signposts, marking crossroads, illuminating the path of life. "Your ears shall hear a word behind you, saying, 'This is the way, walk in it,' whenever you turn to the right hand or whenever you turn to the left" (Isaiah 30:21).

John Newton knew that he had received such a word of warning. He realized that if he chose to ignore it, he had no one to blame but himself.

Such has always been the pattern of the Lord's dealings with humankind. Not only does He personally superintend our situations with vigilance and care, He actually *speaks* to us in the midst of them. "It is the nature of God to speak," writes A. W. Tozer. "The whole Bible supports this idea. God is speaking. Not God spoke, but God *is speaking*. He is, by His nature, continuously articulate. He fills the world with His speaking voice."[3]

For since the creation of the world His invisible attributes are clearly seen, being understood by the things that are made, even His eternal power and Godhead, so that they are without excuse.
ROMANS 1:20

This is why theologian Francis Schaeffer insists that genuine Christian faith is something more than wishful thinking or a blind leap in the dark. Faith, for the biblical believer, is a *response* to the living, speaking, entreating, informing, and warning Word of God. It is not a question of dropping over the side of a cliff in a fog on the mere chance of landing on a projecting outcrop of rock. Instead, it's a matter of listening to the Voice that emerges from the mist and says, "I have lived in these mountains . . . and I know every foot of them. I assure you that ten feet below you there is a ledge."[4]

Our task, like Newton's, is to hear and obey—always remembering that "we are not in our own keeping," but that "He who restored the ring . . . vouchsafes to keep it."[5] For whether the message reaches us through dreams, which may occasionally be "sent to admonish or inform;" or whether, as Newton himself thought far more likely, it comes by the light of the Holy Spirit, "which enables [us] to understand and to love the Scriptures." Whatever the details of the

17

case, the Word will always be accompanied by a full complement of enlivening, empowering grace:

So shall My word be that goes forth from My mouth; it shall not return to Me void, but it shall accomplish what I please, and it shall prosper in the thing for which I sent it. ISAIAH 55:11

WARNING GRACE
God has provided us clues for the journey.

Set me as a seal upon your heart,
as a seal upon your arm; for love
is as strong as death. . . .
Many waters cannot quench love,
nor can the floods drown it.

<small>SONG OF SOLOMON 8:6-7</small>

RESTRAINING GRACE

One hand in the rigging, the other shading his eyes against the glare of the setting sun, John Newton, able seaman, leaned out over the bulwarks and hung above the splash of the waves, watching the coast of England slip away beneath the stern of the HMS *Harwich*.

He groaned and covered his face. Pressed into service with the Royal Navy! Seized and hauled off like a common criminal! Thrust into the dungeonlike hold of a man-o'-war! And all because of his own recklessness and stupidity!

19

Still clinging to the shrouds, he turned and looked up at the quarterdeck. Captain Carteret stood at the rail, deep in conversation with the mate, his cocked blue hat pulled low over his forehead, his hands clasped firmly behind his back. John's face burned at the sight of the man who had stripped him of his rank and ordered him publicly whipped. True, he *had* attempted to desert. But he couldn't help feeling harshly used.

Swinging himself back on deck, he stooped and drew his seaman's knife from his boot. Fingering the worn wooden handle, he shot another glance at the captain. *It would be so easy,* he thought. *So easy to slip up behind him and slide the blade between his ribs.* And why not? What did he have left to lose?

And then it hit him. *Mary.* He'd never see Mary again if he got himself strung up by the yardarm. More than that, he couldn't bear that she should remember him as a murderer and mutineer when he was gone. Biting his lip, he dropped the knife back into his boot and turned again to the sea.

The coast of Britain was long gone, lost in a haze of mist between ocean and sky. He leaned against the bulwark and stared unseeing into the iron-gray troughs and ridges of the sea, his heart a cold and heavy lump of sinking lead. He pictured his body sinking with it into the abyss, drawn down by its weight into the depths, filling slowly with the frigid salt water, dropping at last with a dull thud on the lightless bottom. It would be over quickly—he couldn't swim a lick—a relatively painless end to this misery of floating in-carceration, this agony of restless tossing between heaven and earth.

With both hands he laid hold of the ropes and pulled himself up. Balancing precipitously on the rail, he heard the words of Lord Shaftesbury's *The Moralists, A Philosophical Rhapsody* flit through his mind. If those words were true, if the tenets of organized religion were nothing but the invention of narrow human minds, then he need fear no punishment, no judgment beyond his own sovereign self-determination. He shut his eyes and let go with one hand.

But Mary! Again he saw the brightness of her eyes, the smoothness of her cheek, the blush at the base of her neck. Again he pictured the curve of her mouth, the fullness of her red lips, the freshness of the curls on her forehead.

With a start, he opened his eyes and gaped at the turbulent sea. It was as if a hand had seized him from behind. Gasping, he tottered backward and fell upon the deck.

* * * * *

One of the most appealing things about the history of John Newton's life is that, alongside narratives of youthful wanderings, adventures in exotic lands, perils on the high seas, and a dramatic conversion account, it contains a great love story. It's even possible to argue that romance formed the heart and soul of Newton's spiritual pilgrimage, the hub upon which his transforming experience of grace revolved.

Back in England after his voyage to the Mediterranean, John made a beeline for the home of Mary Catlett. By his own account, Mary was the single point of light in his darkness, and he was drawn to her like a moth to the flame. Once in her presence, he found it virtually impossible to tear himself away and lingered several weeks in Chatham, disappointing and angering his father in the process. As it turned out, he would have reasons of his own for regretting his prolonged sojourn in Kent.

Leaving the Catletts's home at the leisurely and unwary pace of a moonstruck lover, John was apprehended in February 1744 by Lieutenant Thomas Ruffin's press-gang, hustled aboard the tender *Betsy*, and enrolled as part of the crew of the 976-ton warship HMS *Harwich* under the command of Captain Philip Carteret. For Newton, this turn of events was like a sentence of death. The *Harwich* was slated for a five-year tour of duty in the East Indies. If he ever made it back to England, would Mary still be waiting for him? "I think nothing I either felt or feared distressed me so much," he wrote, "as to see myself thus forcibly torn away from the object of my affections, under a great improbability of seeing her again. "[1]

Despondency and rage combined within him to create a dangerously explosive mental and emotional cocktail and

John Newton became "capable of anything."[2] An unsuccessful attempt at desertion was followed by demotion and flogging. He abandoned himself to desperate thoughts and terrifying imaginations, contemplating by turns his own suicide and the murder of the captain.

> Whether I looked inward or outward, I could perceive
> nothing but darkness and misery. . . . I cannot express
> with what wishfulness and regret I cast my last looks
> upon the English shore; I kept my eyes fixed upon it
> till, the ship's distance increasing, it sensibly disappeared; and when I could see it no longer, I was
> tempted to throw myself into the sea.[3]

What was it that prevented Newton from acting upon these dark intentions? One thing is certain: It *wasn't* the fading vestiges of his Christian upbringing. "I had not the least fear of God before my eyes," he confessed later, "nor (so far as I can remember) the least sensibility of conscience."[4] No; at this point in time, there was just one thing holding him back from the edge of the abyss: his love for Mary, the same love that would preserve him through so many "dangers, toils, and snares" yet to come.

> When I afterwards made shipwreck of faith, hope,
> and conscience, my love to this person was the only

remaining principle, which in any degree supplied their place; and the bare possibility of seeing her again was the only present and obvious means of re-straining me from the most horrid designs against myself and others.[5]

Here is a thought worth underscoring and highlighting. In the context of the Creator's broader plan for the bond between male and female, it's not too much to say that *true* love between a woman and a man, however tainted by sin or skewed by selfish desire, always carries within itself the seeds of the divine. Lovers, *as lovers*, are to that very extent operating within the parameters of His will and growing in some degree toward His light. This is why Scripture so consistently describes the ultimate meaning of our existence—our relationship with God—in terms of passionate romance (as in Hosea or the Song of Solomon) and marital consummation (as in Ephesians 5:31-32 and Revelation 19:7). Incredible as it may sound, romantic love, as a subset of "the Love that moves the sun and the other stars,"[6] may sometimes have the potential to become a powerful vehicle of redeeming grace in the life of fallen man. At least it worked that way in the experience of John Newton.

Newton's love for Mary really did turn out to be "as strong as death." It stood the test of time and played a pivotal role in the long and complicated process of bringing the prodigal home. In this sense, Mary Catlett was to Newton what Beatrice was to Dante: not *just* a lover, not *just* a vision of female loveliness, but a guardian angel sent to keep him from the brink of destruction and guide his footsteps to heaven.

Late in life, Newton told his friend and biographer Richard Cecil how often in youth he had traveled from London to the top of Shooters Hill in Kent simply to gain a view of the house where Mary lived at the time. "It gratified me even to look toward the spot," he told Cecil, "and this I did always once and sometimes twice a week."

Cecil was astounded. "Why, this is more like one of the vagaries of romance than of real life!" he said.

"True," responded Newton. "But real life has extravagances that would not be permitted to appear in a well written romance."[7]

Indeed it does. Extravagances like the romance of God's restraining grace.

RESTRAINING GRACE

God protects us from ourselves by the power of love.

AFFLICTING GRACE

The air outside the hut shimmered in the humid equatorial heat. The buzzing of the flies and the whine of the mosquitoes mingled confusedly with the painful hum inside his head. Unable to keep still because of the restlessness in his limbs, John tossed from side to side on his reed mat, staring listlessly at the thin vapors rising from the patch of ground outside the door. He would have given anything for something to eat; now that the fever had abated, hunger was gnawing at the pit of his stomach again. But he hadn't the strength to rise, let alone dig for roots in the sand.

By slow degrees, he became aware of a dark figure standing in the doorway.

"You must get up!" said a familiar voice. "The mistress calls!"

"Sury?" he said, raising himself painfully on one elbow. "Is that you?"

Hastening to his bedside, the servant raised him by the armpits and hauled him to his feet. "Lean on me!" he said. "She sent me to say that you must claim what is left of her dinner before it is too late. If you don't get it, the dogs will!"

Inside the big wooden house—the house that John himself had built almost single-handedly—the master's African wife sat at the head of the table, dressed in a European gown of green brocaded silk, flanked on either side by three black slaves. Her face shone like ebony beneath a scarlet turban, and her white teeth flashed in a wide smile as she picked up a plate of scraps and held it out to John.

"Let him go, Sury," she said. "If he wants it, he must come and get it!"

She was a person of some importance in that part of the Guinea coast, or so he had always heard; a daughter of the ruling Bombo family of Sherbro. Here on Plantain Island she was undisputed queen. Even if he hadn't been in such a weakened condition, John could have done nothing to gainsay her in the master's absence. He cursed his bad luck in falling ill at a time like this.

Sury released his grip and nudged the invalid forward.

JOHN NEWTON:
Afflicting Grace

John stumbled, checked himself, and stood wavering. Suddenly all the color bleached out of the walls and furniture. The clothing and the faces of the people went white. The room began to tilt and spin. Bracing himself, John took another tentative step toward the table, then faltered and dropped to one knee. Instantly the room rang with the mistress's high-pitched laughter.

"See how nice and pretty he walks!" she shrieked. The six men at her side began to laugh along, uncertain at first, then with growing zest and enthusiasm. Grinning broadly, she rose from her chair, bent forward, and waggled the plate at arm's length. "Not far now!" she cooed.

Somehow or other, John struggled to his feet. Step by slow step, he fought his way to the table, gazing all the while into her wide-set, deep brown eyes, everything within him painfully straining towards the food. At last the prize was in his hand, but his weakened fingers could not hold it. With a sickening crash, the plate slipped and fell to the floor.

"Too bad!" she cried, clucking her tongue as the dogs descended upon the fragments. "You'll just have to wait until tomorrow!"

* * * * *

"Next to pressing want," wrote John Newton in his *Authentic Narrative*, "nothing sits harder on the mind than scorn and contempt."[1] He had good reason to know. His first two years in Africa were a period of physical deprivation *and* mental anguish beyond anything Newton had yet endured or would ever be required to face again. So intense was his suffering that it nearly killed him. But in the end, he came to see even *this* terrible experience as a manifestation of God's amazing grace.

On board the *Harwich*, torn between thoughts of suicide and his undying love for Mary, John had made a resolution of sorts: "Two things I had determined when at Plymouth: that I would *not* go to India, and that I *would* go to Guinea."[2] In the event, this was precisely what happened, but not in the way young Newton had envisioned or planned. *He* was entertaining "golden dreams" of "improving his fortune" in Africa. Providence had something else in mind.

Unexpectedly discharged from the Royal Navy, John had landed in the service of a slave trader who maintained a lucrative business on Plantain Island, a small spit of land just off the coast of Sierra Leone. Impressed with this merchant's outward prosperity, Newton imagined that in his employ he'd rapidly earn enough money to return to England and ask for Mary's hand in marriage. He had no way of knowing that he was about to be enrolled in a crash course in hardship and affliction.

Soon after his arrival on the island, John fell ill with a devastating "fever," almost certainly a severe case of malaria. His employer, who had been planning a slave-collecting expedition on the mainland, was forced to set off without him. This meant leaving Newton in the care of the master's African common-law wife, a formidable woman known to history only as P. I. (because her name sounded like these two letters pronounced separately).

P. I. quickly conceived a strong prejudice against the young Englishman. At first she reluctantly attended to his needs, but as Newton's illness progressed he was increasingly left on his own. Neglect soon gave way to mistreatment. Insult was heaped upon injury. When at last the sickness left him, she made sport of his weakness and hunger, tantalized him with offers of food, and incited the household servants to pelt him with rocks and limes. Newton's situation didn't improve when the master returned. Falsely accused of stealing, Newton was degraded to a position of servitude, chained to the deck of a boat, and exposed to the elements. Even the lowest slaves pitied him.

In some circles it has become fashionable to edit the opening lines of "Amazing Grace" to read: "Amazing grace! How sweet the sound that saved a *soul* like me." But Newton didn't choose the word "wretch"—*outcast, exile, miserable, homeless wanderer*—carelessly or at random. Because of experiences like Plantain Island, he *felt* profoundly that this particular word epitomized the essence of who and what he was in and of himself, apart from the unmerited mercy of God. In later life, when he looked back over the circumstances that had led him to a living and transforming encounter with divine grace, he saw clearly that "wretchedness" had been a vital and indispensable part of the process. As author Steve Turner puts it, "Plantain Island was to provide the reference point against which he would always measure his spiritual and social progress."[3] To the end of his days, he thought of himself as "John Newton, Clerk, once an infidel and libertine, a servant of slaves in Africa."[4]

Why should this be so? In Newton's position, most of us wouldn't feel particularly inclined to heap blame upon ourselves. If subjected to the kind of mistreatment he received from P. I., our natural response would probably be one of outrage and indignation. *Victim*, not *wretch*, is the word that would spring most readily to our minds. And at a certain level we'd be absolutely right. But as Turner points out, "Newton had a wider angle of vision."[5] He was keenly aware that, from the moment of his release from the *Harwich*, his pride and self-will had been on the upswing—that he had, in fact, become "the willing slave of every evil."[6]

> From this time [of my discharge from the Royal Navy], I was exceedingly vile indeed, little if anything short of that animated description of an almost irrecoverable state which we have in 2 Peter 2:14.

I not only sinned with a high hand myself, but made it my study to tempt and seduce others upon every occasion.[7]

To put it bluntly, Newton knew that he needed to be taken down a peg or two, set free from bondage to his own sensuality and rebellion. And affliction was to become one of the most important means of effecting his release.

In retrospect, Newton interpreted Plantain Island as "a needful memento of the wages of sin." He still had a long way to go before he would reach the place of heartfelt repentance and conversion. But even at this preliminary stage, the weakening effects of sickness and suffering had done him a world of good. "My haughty heart was now brought down. . . . I had lost the fierceness which fired me when on board the *Harwich*, and which made me capable of the most desperate attempts."[8]

It was just another step along the pathway of a long and tortuous pilgrimage. But in the end it proved to be extremely important. If John Newton had never come face-to-face with the reality of his own wretchedness, he might have destroyed himself long before he had a chance to receive the gift of forgiveness and life.

Many of us today desperately need to learn the same lesson—that it is the meek and lowly, not the self-confident and self-assertive, who will inherit the kingdom of God; and that "The Lord is near to those who have a broken heart, and saves such as have a contrite spirit" (Psalm 34:18).

AFFLICTING GRACE
It is by God's mercy that we are brought low.

*If I take the wings of the morning,
and dwell in the uttermost parts of
the sea, even there Your hand shall
lead me, and Your right hand
shall hold me.*

PSALM 139:9-10

PRESERVING GRACE

Seated on boxes and bales, the four sailors lifted their faces, white in the moonlight, and gave full attention to the master of ceremonies. John Newton, presiding over the group from behind a large barrel he'd dragged on to the deck for the occasion, uncorked a bottle of gin and poured its contents into a large abalone shell.

"A drinking bowl fit for the likes of you!" he cried. "And now for a toast!"

"A toast!" laughed the others. "To the *Greyhound!*"

"To Captain Gother!"

"To frolic, merriment, and mirth!"

"No!" roared John, raising a hand for silence. "To the first man who can drain the bowl at a draught: May he rot in hell and his substance go down to Davy Jones!"

Again they howled with glee. "And who should that be but *you*, you old reprobate?" said one.

"Aye!" cried another. "Let the host be first to sample the vintage!"

John cocked a defiant eye at them; slowly and deliberately, he lifted the shell to his lips and emptied it. Then, to a rousing chorus of cheers, he refilled the bowl and handed it to the man on his right.

Around the circle it went, then, again and again returning to the barrel to be replenished. Bottle after bottle of gin and rum went into the shell and down the sailors' gullets. Once, twice, three times John drained the cup to the dregs, always to louder and more raucous acclaim. His stomach burned. He felt the fire rising to his brain.

"A hornpipe, Billy!" he shouted. Billy, who was now barely capable of putting bow to string, produced a fiddle and began drunkenly to play as John danced madly about the deck, leaping and kicking while the others cried "hurrah!" and clapped in time with the music. Spurred by their enthusiasm, John threw himself into the performance with ever greater zeal until at last he stumbled over the barrel and fell heavily against the railing. Off flew his hat, over the side of the ship, down into the dark waters of the Gabon River. John pulled himself up and hung over the rail, watching it float away on the swift-running tide.

"Not to worry!" he cried, catching sight of the ship's boat, a bobbing and weaving shape at the end of a moonlit cable. "I'll go after it—in the launch!" Squinting, he shook his muddled head and wondered vaguely how far off the small craft lay. It looked like an easy jump. He gripped the rail and prepared to jump; but in that very instant someone grasped him by the collar and forcibly yanked him back.

"Fool!" said a voice in his ear. "That boat's twenty feet off! Do you mean to drown yourself?"

Dizzy and stunned, John turned to look his rescuer in the face. Billy was still sawing away at the fiddle. The rest of the company lay sprawled listlessly across the deck.

"But my hat!" he spluttered angrily. And then he collapsed against the bulwark and dissolved into a fit of uncontrolled laughter.

* * * * *

Among other things, the song "Amazing Grace" celebrates the hymn writer's safe deliverance from "many dangers, toils, and snares." As even the most casual student of Newton's life must recognize, the words are poignantly autobiographical.

We've already seen how John's love for Mary prevented him from committing murder and suicide. We've also considered the beneficial effects of sickness and suffering upon his reckless and haughty spirit. But there are many other examples of God's protecting grace operating in Newton's life. One might almost say that divine *preservation* is the single most important thread running through the early chapters of his story. The scene re-narrated above is a memorable case in point.

Released from the miseries he'd endured in the service of P. I. and her husband, John found work with another slave trader in a different part of the island, a man of a kinder and more congenial temper. Newton's fortunes improved at once, at least on the physical and material plane. It wasn't long before he was feeling his oats again and learning to enjoy the African way of life. "Here," he wrote, "I began to be wretch enough to think myself happy."[1]

So happy was he, in fact, that he found it difficult to leave when a ship dispatched by his father's friend Joseph Manesty came looking for him. Captain Anthony Gother, commanding officer of the *Greyhound*, finally managed to persuade John with a little white lie: He told him that a wealthy relative had recently died, leaving him a legacy of four hundred pounds a year. Newton swallowed the bait, believing that this was his chance to return home and marry the girl of his dreams.

The incident of the drunken dance and lost hat took place

on board the *Greyhound*. Though hardship and affliction had left a deep and lasting impact on John's life, his character was far from being fully reformed. "I was no further changed than a tiger tamed by hunger," he said later. "Remove the occasion and he will be as wild as ever."[2] It's a note we'll hear sounded again and again; in Newton's case, genuine moral and spiritual change was always slow and gradual, usually a matter of "three steps forward, two steps back."

As the *Greyhound* made her way up and down the African coast collecting gold, ivory, dyer's wood, and beeswax, John gradually fell back into his old ways. His speech became peppered with blasphemous language, and swearing. And he filled his waking hours devising clever arguments against the tenets of Christianity.

He took up drinking, too, even though he'd never had a taste for alcohol. "Sometimes I would promote a drinking bout for a frolic's sake, as I termed it: for though I did not love the liquor, I was sold to do iniquity and delighted in mischief."[3] It was during one of these "abominable frolics" that his hat went overboard and he was miraculously saved from leaping after it and drowning when "somebody caught hold of [his] clothes behind, and pulled [him] back"—exactly who, it's difficult to say, since his drinking companions were too intoxicated to come to his rescue, "and the rest of the ship's company were asleep."[4]

Nor was this the first—or the last—time that Newton was strangely delivered from death by circumstances beyond his control. As a child, he had been thrown from a horse and only narrowly missed being impaled on the sharp stakes of a newly cut hedgerow. Not long afterward, he arrived too late to join some friends who were rowing out to visit a man-o'-war anchored in the Thames; the boys' boat overturned and several of them drowned. Later, on a night that would change the course of Newton's life, he would be ordered below by the captain, only to learn that the sailor who replaced him was immediately swept overboard.

Taken together, these and a number of similar events almost seem to suggest a pattern. Anyone would suppose that *Somebody* had reasons for wanting John Newton alive, in spite of his reckless folly, his disdain for the truth of God, and his stiff-necked resistance to the operation of grace in his life.

Newton's experience underscores a principle that we must never forget. It is not because of our own goodness or merit that we are kept alive on this earth, not even for the briefest moment. Every breath we take is a gift of undeserved grace. Every heartbeat is granted to us out of "the riches of His goodness, forbearance, and longsuffering," all of which are calculated to "[lead us] to repentance" (Romans 2:4; see also 2 Peter 3:9). As Newton himself wrote, "We cannot at present conceive how much we owe to the guardian care of

40

Divine Providence, that any of us are preserved in peace and safety for a single day in such a world as this."[5]

But there's another side to this coin. Newton's story also provides a powerful illustration of the truth that our times are in God's hands (Psalm 31:15), and that, until His purposes for our lives have been fulfilled, divine protection renders us *virtually immortal*. "[Man's] days are determined," says Job, "[and] the number of his months is with You; You have appointed his limits, so that he cannot pass" (Job 14:5).

Here we find cause for both sober reflection *and* great joy. There is comfort and assurance in the realization that *nothing* can touch us apart from our Father's will. But there is also an impulse to serious self-examination in the thought that *every* moment could be our last—our final opportunity to turn and seek His face.

This, too, is a manifestation of His incredible, amazing grace.

PRESERVING GRACE
We are never beyond the reach of God's protective care.

> *No one can come to Me unless the Father who sent Me draws him; and I will raise him up at the last day.*
>
> JOHN 6:44

ILLUMINATING GRACE

What if these things should be true?

John shut the book—a worn copy of George Stanhope's translation of *The Imitation of Christ*—and pushed the thought aside. The air inside the cabin was close and oppressive despite the cold North Atlantic air on the other side of the creaking timbers. He crept into his berth and pulled his cap down over his face.

This wasn't the first time he'd dipped into Thomas à Kempis. Except for the New Testament and a collection of

Bishop Beveridge's sermons, the *Imitation* was all the reading material he had on board. He'd always regarded it as a mere curiosity, a mildly interesting way to beguile a dull evening. Never before had it left the least impression upon him. But now he could not put its ringing sentences out of his mind.

> Vanity of vanities and all is vanity, except to love God and to serve only Him.

Above deck the wind was singing in the rigging. Below in the darkness Newton tossed and turned in his bunk. At last the words of the book lulled him into an uneasy sleep.

> It is vanity to chase after what the world says you should want. . . . People who live in the world on its terms instead of on God's stain their conscience and lose God's grace.

He woke with a gasp and a violent start. From above came an explosive blast like the bursting of a great sheet of canvas. This was followed by a flash of blinding white light. The ship lurched and her sides shuddered. A torrent of frigid air and foaming brine came pouring down the hatchway. John jumped from his bunk and found himself standing waist-deep in icy water.

"A nor'wester!" came the frantic cries of the crew. "All hands! All hands!"

JOHN NEWTON:
Illuminating Grace

"Get below, Newton, and fetch me a knife!" shouted the captain as John came tearing up the ladder. He turned and splashed back into the hold while another sailor went topside in his stead. Snatching a blade from his sea chest, John dashed to the hatch and emerged on deck just in time to see the man who had taken his place swept away by the force of the sea.

> It is vanity to wish for a long life and to care little about a good life. . . . It is vanity to focus only on your present life and not to look ahead to your future life.

From three in the morning till noon the next day, John Newton labored at the pumps, lashed tightly to a beam. He was haunted by the words of the book, bound not only to the beam, but also to the sinking weight of his own unrepented sin. On every side, men wept and raged and cursed the God of heaven. *Why*, he wondered, *are they so obtuse, so unaware of the everlasting darkness looming over their heads?* And why had it taken him so long to awaken to thoughts of his soul's eternal destiny?

"What progress at the pumps?" asked the captain, as John, nearly dead with cold and fatigue, passed him on his way to a well-deserved rest.

John stopped, brushed the hair from his eyes, and looked the captain in the face.

"If this will not do, sir," he said quietly, "the Lord have mercy on us."

* * * * *

There is so little about ourselves over which we exert any kind of control. We can't add an inch to our stature (Matthew 6:27) or turn a hair of our heads either white or black (not *permanently*, at any rate—and not without artificial aids! Matthew 5:36). We don't get to choose our parents or our relatives. We have no idea why we were brought into the world at this particular time and in this particular place. Even our own thoughts and emotions defy comprehension and direction. Like flitting fireflies, they come and go, flashing out of darkness into light, vanishing without explanation. We can barely hold them long enough to get a good look at them.

Least of all are we able to govern our own sensitivity to spiritual things: to dictate the nature and timing of our responses to God, or to control our reactions to His persistent bids for our attention, and tireless overtures of love. John Newton was deeply and keenly aware of this truth. It was brought home to him in an unforgettable way; he later termed his conversion as an "apparent conversion"—"apparent" because he tended to distrust his own perceptions and also because he viewed redemption as an ongoing, progressive affair. But while he was convinced that Christian transformation is not accomplished in a day, he also knew that it *must* have a beginning. And that beginning, Newton firmly believed, always arises at a point *external* to ourselves. It reaches down and seizes us *from above*, with or without the exercise of our understanding and will.

> The tenth (that is, in the present style, the twenty-first) of March, is a day much to be remembered by me, and I have never suffered it to pass wholly unnoticed since the year 1748. On that day the Lord sent from on high, and delivered me out of deep waters.[1]

On that date the *Greyhound* was scudding rapidly over the North Atlantic before a stiff westerly wind. Newton and his shipmates fully expected to complete the homeward leg of their journey in record time. They had no way of knowing that the "hard gale" would rapidly develop into a deadly tempest. Nor did John suspect that the course of his life would be radically altered in the heart of the ensuing storm.

The night before the onset of the maelstrom Newton picked up a volume with which he had become intimately familiar during the course of this voyage: Thomas à Kempis's fifteenth-century devotional classic, *The Imitation of Christ*. Religion meant nothing to him at the time, of course, but he was an incurable bookworm who found it impossible to survive the tedious hours at sea without some kind of printed material in hand. So he opened the *Imitation* and began to read:

"Anyone who follows me shall not walk in darkness,"
says the Lord. These are the words of Christ, and by
them we are reminded that we must imitate His life
and His ways if we are to be truly enlightened and set
free from the darkness of our own hearts.[2]

He had probably read these sentences many times while
aboard the *Greyhound*, always with the same air of cool, de-
tached indifference. But on this occasion they struck him
with a strange new force. As if from out of nowhere, a
thought crashed in upon him like a peal of thunder: *What if
these words should be true?*

Why had this question never occurred to him before? He
couldn't say. He couldn't even grasp why it should present
itself to him now, or how it could possibly arise in a mind
like *his*, a mind that had for so long flagrantly opposed the
Christian message. The only thing he knew was that, without
being invited, it had suddenly taken full and instant possession of him. It didn't take long for Newton to concede that
the words of the book not only were true, but that they had
huge implications for the future direction of his life.

Did Newton arrive at this conclusion by virtue of his own
wisdom and intelligence? Was he persuaded by the logic of
Thomas à Kempis? Or could it be that he was brought to his
senses by the terrors of the storm that so quickly followed

the rereading of this familiar passage? Apparently the answer is "none of the above."

> No temporal dispensations can reach the heart, unless the Lord Himself applies them. My companions in danger were either quite unaffected, or soon forgot it all, but it was not so with me: not that I was any wiser or better than they, but because the Lord was pleased to vouchsafe me peculiar mercy.[3]

In the upshot, John Newton was plucked from the depths and transformed by the power of love. Despite his stubborn recalcitrance, he was seized from above and redirected by the hand of Another. His blind eyes were opened; like Saul of Tarsus, he was *made* to see. Most importantly, all of this happened to him quite apart from his own desires and without his conscious consent. It was as if he were the victim—the blessed, fortunate victim—of a redeeming and rescuing force beyond his control.

What about *you*? Do you know yet what it means to become the beneficiary of "peculiar mercy"? Have you experienced what the biblical writers had in mind when they declared that not only *salvation*, but even the enlightenment that leads to *repentance* is a free, unmerited *gift* (Acts 5:31; Ephesians 2:8)? Have you, like John Newton, ever heard the Savior say, "You did not choose Me, but *I chose you*" (John 15:16)?

If not, you're in for a ride—the most marvelous, wonderful, and amazingly gracious ride of your life.

ILLUMINATING GRACE

It is by grace that we are enabled to see our need of grace.

Then after fourteen years I went up again to Jerusalem.

GALATIANS 2:1

DELAYING GRACE

"Dearly beloved, we are gathered together here in the sight of God, and in the face of this congregation, to join together this man, John Newton, and this woman, Mary Catlett, in holy matrimony."

The minister's voice glanced off the stone pillars and hung ringing beneath the high vault of St. Margaret's Church. Stealing a sidewise glance at Mary, John saw the light of the candles and the colors of the stained glass reflected on her face. He pinched himself. Could it be that the dream was really coming true at last?

"This is an honorable estate, instituted by God in the time

of man's innocency, signifying unto us the mystical union that is betwixt Christ and His Church. . . ."

More than seven years had passed since he, a gawky adolescent bound for mischief and misadventure on the high seas, had stood tongue-tied and abashed in her presence, a girl not yet fourteen years of age. By his own account, it had been love at first sight; but it was not for that reason a fickle or fleeting love. Through all the widely varied scenes that followed that first meeting—the drunken follies and unrestrained blasphemies, the hard labors and deadly dangers, the terrors of sea and storm, the drama of his miraculous conversion—Mary's image had never once faded from his waking thoughts. He pinched himself again, but the vision did not vanish.

"Wilt thou, John Newton, have this woman, Mary Catlett, to be thy wedded wife, to live together after God's ordinance in the holy estate of matrimony?"

He blinked. Had the question been addressed to him? Of course! But so dreamlike was the moment, and so lost was he in his own reflections that he found himself stumbling over the answer: "I will!" he said at last. "Indeed I will!"

He could see Mary regarding him playfully out of the corner of her eye, a smile tugging at the corners of her mouth. This too, he knew, was mercy and grace. The waiting had been hard, terribly hard—unbearable at times. How often had he thought of her when in the throes of a burning fever or while under the cruel and oppressive hand of P. I.? How many times had he checked himself in some mad course simply in hopes of seeing her again? And yet it was clear to him now that the fulfillment of his longings could not have been granted an hour sooner. He felt a lump rising in his throat as he considered the implications. To think that his young and unschooled affections should have been so fortunate as to light upon her when his head could have been turned by any pretty face!

At the edge of conscious thought he heard the voice of Mary repeating the solemn promise: "I will." And now he was holding her hand and placing the ring upon her finger: "With this ring I thee wed, with my body I thee worship, and with all my worldly goods I thee endow: In the name of the Father, and of the Son, and of the Holy Ghost. Amen."

It was the first of February. Though the air outside was heavy with frost, the returning light, green and cold, was already lingering later in the afternoon sky. Linking his arm in hers, John passed through the vestibule, crossed the church threshold, and walked out into the streets of Rochester. Spring could not be far off.

* * * * *

It has been said many times that we live in an age of impatience, an era in which no one is willing to *wait* for anything.

Trite as it sounds after the umpteenth repetition, the observation is still profoundly true. Nor is it without good reason that we hear it reiterated so often. For those who wait upon the Lord renew their strength (Isaiah 40:31); and those who will *not* wait *miss out*.

> If a mariner is surprised by a storm, and after one night spent in jeopardy, is presently brought safe into port; though he may rejoice in his deliverance, it will not affect him so sensibly, as if, after being tempest-tossed for a long season, and experiencing a great number and variety of hair-breadth escapes, he at last gains the desired haven.[1]

It will not affect him so sensibly. In other words, he will not *feel* it as sharply. Just as the one who has been forgiven much loves much (Luke 7:47), so he who *waits* to receive the prize cherishes it all the more intensely. Here, to a great extent, is the source of the depth and richness of John Newton's spiritual life.

Interestingly enough, it was not in storms and tempests that Newton encountered this principle in its most affecting form. Instead, his greatest discoveries with regard to the benefits of waiting were made in the context of his protracted romance with Mary Catlett. It was here that he tasted the sweetness of love deferred until the appropriate moment;

and it was here that he was most forcibly compelled to stand in awe of the Lord's impeccable timing.

Arriving in Liverpool after his life-changing journey across the Atlantic, John had gone almost immediately to Kent to renew his suit for Mary's hand. He went in fear and trepidation; for while most of the *practical* obstacles to their marriage had evaporated by this time, he believed that with Mary herself he still stood "at as great an uncertainty as on the first day I saw her."

Apparently his suspicions were not ill-founded. The interview was an awkward affair. So keen were his anxieties, so strong his feelings, that Newton fumbled his words, muffed his proposal, and went away under the conviction that his efforts had "availed very little."

But he didn't give up. Back in Liverpool, where he was already preparing for another voyage to Guinea—a voyage that would keep him abroad for the greater part of the next two years—he resorted to his most effective weapon: the written word. Pen in hand, he again took up his earnest but tender assault upon the heart of his beloved. This time the results were more favorable: In response to John's letter, Mary agreed that they should be wed as soon as he returned to England.

It's not hard to imagine the flood of emotions that must have overtaken him as he stood with his bride at the altar of

St. Margaret's Church in Rochester on February 1, 1750. It had been a long, hard, and uncertain road, but John could see clearly that the hand of God had been at work in the details. He knew that he and Mary had been favored and blessed in many ways, not least by being asked to *wait*.

> The satisfaction I have found in this union, you will suppose, has been greatly heightened by reflections on the former disagreeable contrasts I had passed through. . . . The long delay I met with was likewise a mercy; for, had I succeeded a year or two sooner, before the Lord was pleased to change my heart, we must have been mutually unhappy, even as to the present life. Surely goodness and mercy have followed me all my days.[2]

What if this element of delay had been eliminated from the history of John and Mary's courtship? What if he had succeeded in persuading her to join him, heart and hand, *prior* to his conversion at sea, while still a proud, hardened, self-willed, and brazen blasphemer? Would the marriage have lasted? If it had, would the partners have lived to regret it? Only the God of goodness and mercy knows. Only *He* had the power to avert such a disaster by requiring the lovers to wait.

Goodness and mercy. These are the twin dogs that hounded Moses and the children of Israel all the way across the Sinai desert. They were Abraham's constant companions, from the moment he heard the words "I will make you a great nation" (Genesis 12:2) until the day his son Isaac was born, almost a quarter century later (Genesis 21:1-3). They were hot on Jacob's heels throughout the twenty-one years of his labors in the household of Laban. They must have felt like an almost palpable presence when Paul of Tarsus, nearly a decade and a half after the vision that designated him apostle to the Gentiles (Acts 22:21), finally saw his ministry approved by the leaders of the church in Jerusalem (Acts 15:2).

"It is merciful in the Lord to disappoint our plans and to cross our wishes," wrote Newton.[3] But it is equally merciful of Him to restore those dreams, like beauty for ashes, at the proper time. This amazing grace dogs *all* our steps through *all* the convoluted passages of our earthly lives.

Oh, that we had eyes to see it—and patience to *wait* unruffled for the fulfillment of the promise it conceals!

DELAYING GRACE
Though He asks us to wait, God is never late.

For now we see in a mirror, dimly, but then face to face. Now I know in part, but then I shall know just as I also am known.

1 CORINTHIANS 13:12

GROWING GRACE

Tacking before a steady southwest wind, rolling heavily with the weight of her precious cargo—"black gold" from the Guinea coast, slaves for the prosperous planters of the West Indies—the *African* held firm on her zigzagging course across the Atlantic. It was still early in the Middle Passage. Sierra Leone lay but a day behind the stern. As yet there had not been time for the stench in the hold to become unbearable. The clouds were high, the breeze fair, the swell of the sea gentle and propitious.

Captain John Newton stood on the quarterdeck, savoring the salt air, contemplating the prospect of a leisurely voyage to

St. Kitts. He smiled at the thought of morning prayers, afternoons reading Caesar and Euclid, scriptural studies in the evenings, and public worship with the crew every Lord's Day. It had been hard to leave Mary, of course, terribly hard. Yet the life of a merchant captain was not without compensations. And with his interest firmly established upon the trade, he need not worry about his ability to support a wife. Glowing with the fervor of his newfound faith, Newton offered up thanks to the Lord his Provider. The future looked bright.

"Isn't it grand?" he said to the first mate, who stood scanning the horizon through a spyglass. "The expanded heavens. The wide ocean. The wonders of God in the great deep. I know of no calling more conducive to advancement in the spiritual life than that of a seafarer! And to think that—"

Newton was interrupted by a sudden crash and a low rumble, followed by the shouts of sailors and a chorus of muffled cries—the sounds of a disturbance below.

The mate shut the spyglass with a snap. "Sir?" he said with a questioning glance.

"You must go and see what the trouble's about," said the captain with a sigh. "I *do* dislike chains and shackles. But necessity is necessity and business is business. Use kindness as far as it is humanly possible. I mean to run this ship by Christian principles."

"Aye, sir," said the mate, turning to go.

JOHN NEWTON:
Growing Grace

In his cabin, Captain Newton seated himself at the table, picked up a worn copy of Caesar's *Gallic War*, and began to read aloud. "*Gallia est omnis divisa in partis tris*—all of Gaul is divided into three parts."

Instantly he was struck with a pang of conscience. As if out of nowhere, a flood of conviction overwhelmed him. A shaft of divine light pierced him to the soul. He tossed the book aside, bowed his head upon folded hands, and began to pray aloud.

"O Lord," he cried, "forgive Thy servant! By Thine abundant grace Thou hast delivered me out of deep waters and preserved my life! Yet here I sit, despising the incomparable gift, exchanging the pearl of great price for a mess of pottage! How can I have been so blind? O Lord, pardon my sin and redirect my wayward heart!"

Looking up from his prayer, Newton took pen and journal in hand. *Resolved*, he wrote, *from this day forth, not another moment to be frittered away on the Latin classics or any other sinful and frivolous works of pagan literature. Henceforth all of my reading time to be devoted entirely to the holy and eternal Word of God.*

Below, the hull of the *African* rang with the frightened cries of her human freight.

* * * * *

For insight into John Newton's unique perspective on the "normal Christian life" there is no better place to turn than

Jesus' parable of the growing seed. It's a disarmingly simple story. A man sows seed in his field. While he goes about his business, the seed sprouts and grows. But it doesn't happen all at once: "For the earth yields crops by itself: first the blade, then the head, after that the full grain in the head" (Mark 4:26-29).

This was one of Newton's favorite passages of Scripture. It was foundational to his concept of the "three stages" of a believer's spiritual development: "the blade, the ear, and the full corn in the ear."[1] As such, it is the key to the compassion and tenderness that later characterized his ministry as a pastor and spiritual counselor. Newton was always infinitely patient with struggling Christians. Because he took Jesus' formula for growth seriously, he didn't expect the seed of grace to produce a full crop in a single night. Instead, he let it germinate and flower in the hearts of others as he had seen it unfold in his own—slowly, gradually, and at its own pace.

The scene narrated above, while purely fictional in its details, is nevertheless based solidly on the plain and unadorned facts of John Newton's experience as a newly converted, born-again believer. From our twenty-first-century point of view, it's a story filled with glaring inconsistencies. For while he was constant in prayer, exacting in self-examination, and uncompromising in the pursuit of personal holiness, Newton nevertheless entered upon the pathway of

JOHN NEWTON:
Growing Grace

Christian discipleship while actively engaged in one of the vilest and most horrific "businesses" ever known to mankind: the slave trade. Within two years of his life-changing experience in the midst of that storm (in 1750), a friend and patron made John captain of his own slave ship, an occupation at which he labored—with great financial gain—for the next five years.

To most modern readers this is absolutely scandalous. Newton, the enthusiastic young believer, walked with Jesus while trafficking in the bodies and souls of human beings. He studied the Scriptures while selling Africans into bondage. He prayed and worshiped God in his cabin while men and women languished in chains in the hold of his ship. And he seems to have done all this without giving the matter a second thought. When asked later in life whether he had ever struggled with doubts about the legitimacy of this line of work, he answered, "I felt it very ineligible, but I had no scruple of the lawfulness of it."[2] Indeed, he suffered greater pangs of unease and guilt over his tendency to "waste time" on Latin and geometry than he did over the question of slavery.

What makes this all the more interesting is that it is completely at variance with certain popular conceptions of the history of Newton's life. Many people seem to assume that he wrote the hymn "Amazing Grace" about his "rejection of the slave trade and how his eyes had been opened to its evil."[3] "Something happened," says folksinger Arlo Guthrie, "a storm or something, and he promised God that if he was allowed to live he would turn his life around. And he did. He took the people home, sailed back to England, and started writing songs."[4] But that's *not* the way it happened.

The truth of the matter is that Newton continued in the slave trade until a stroke forced him to give up the seafaring life. The revulsion that he *later* came to feel toward the institution of slavery emerged only slowly and gradually, first under the influence of the poet William Cowper, and then as an aspect of his association with William Wilberforce. Thirty years after leaving the industry, Newton wrote an essay, *Thoughts upon the African Slave Trade* (1788), in which he expressed deep remorse over his participation in "a commerce so iniquitous, so cruel, so oppressive, [and] so destructive."[5] Thus it came about that the "blade" of young Newton's uninformed zeal *did* eventually yield a "full crop" of clear-sighted Christian humanitarianism. But like Rome, this powerful, life-changing conviction was not built in a day. Instead, it was a product of *growing grace.*

Perhaps Newton had that sort of grace in mind when he wrote the following description of a mature believer:

His own heart, and the knowledge he has acquired of the snares of the world, and the subtlety of Satan,

64

teach him to make all due allowances.[6] . . . He believes
and feels his own weakness and unworthiness, and
lives upon the grace and pardoning love of his Lord.
This gives him an habitual tenderness and gentleness
of spirit. Humbled under a sense of much forgiveness
to himself, he finds it easy to forgive others.[7]

Bruce Hindmarsh expands on this theme. "The whole thrust
of Newton's teaching," he says, "emphasized the progressive, lifelong nature of the believer's growth in holiness.
Against any form of evangelicalism which overemphasizes
climactic conversion to the exclusion of the long-term experience of Christian growth, Newton lays out a road map for a
life of convertedness."[8]

*All due allowances. Long-term experience. A road map for a life of
convertedness.* Don't we *all* have a desperate need for these
by-products of the operation of grace? Newton "found it easy
to forgive others," but some of *us* have a tendency to heap
blame on our slow-growing brothers and sisters. Others lose
patience with *themselves* when old habits die hard and the Christian life doesn't progress according to schedule. Still others
find gnats of inconsistency in the lives of past believers like
Newton but swallow the camels of contemporary cultural as-
sumptions whole. On the surface, we look about as ridiculous
and hopeless as the pious young slave trader himself.

But it is not so. For the Lord knows us intimately, and it is by His grace alone that we are carried, each according to the measure of our readiness and need, from one plateau of insight and understanding to the next. Under His loving and watchful eye the good work begun in our souls *will* be brought to completion (Philippians 1:6). The blade *will* develop a head, and the head *will* produce a rich harvest of grain.

Therefore do not lose heart; for "He who calls you is faithful, who also will do it" (1 Thessalonians 5:24).

GROWING GRACE

Consistently holy character is the fruit of abiding in Christ.

[God] comforts us in all our tribulation, that we may be able to comfort those who are in any trouble, with the comfort with which we ourselves are comforted by God.

2 Corinthians 1:4

LONG-SUFFERING GRACE

"Now, Mr. Cowper," said the Reverend John Newton, dragging his chair closer to the fender and wrapping a woolen shawl around his shoulders. "Let's see what you've managed to come up with this week."

William Cowper sighed, his breath escaping upward in a white plume. It had been one of the harshest Decembers on record, and the air inside the room was frigid despite the fire on the grate. Reluctantly, the long-faced poet produced a disorderly sheaf of papers from his overcoat and laid it on the table.

"Just this," he said, taking a sheet from the top of the pile. "It's my last," he added ominously.

Newton raised an eyebrow. It had been a long while since his melancholy friend had suffered a serious bout of depression. Adjusting his spectacles with a feeling of vague anxiety, the vicar began to read:

> *God moves in a mysterious way His wonders to perform;*
> *He plants His footsteps in the sea and rides upon the storm . . .*

"Excellent, as usual," observed Newton. "Though I see the old preoccupation with storms has raised its head again." He shot the poet a questioning glance.

"God knows I've seen more than my fair share," said Cowper. "Like you, John. Unlike you, I haven't been able to leave them on the ocean."

Newton laughed, a thoughtful, gentle laugh. "Squalls have a way of following a man ashore, I find," he said. "As reflected in this, *my* latest effort." He held up a paper for Cowper's inspection. "What do you think?"

Cowper read the lines aloud:

> *Through many dangers, toils, and snares I have already come;*
> *'Tis grace has brought me safe thus far, and grace will lead me home.*

"It's like you," Cowper mused. "Hopeful and bright. I only wish I might share your sense of good expectation."

JOHN NEWTON:
Long-Suffering Grace

Newton peered at his companion in the firelight, his concerns now fully aroused. "But you *can*, William," he said earnestly. "You *do*." They had been over this ground a hundred times before; and yet on this occasion there was a shadow on his companion's face that warned him to tread softly. "The promise belongs to *you*, as it does to *all* who believe. Surely you know that as well as I do?"

"I did once," said Cowper. "Or I *thought* I did." He rose and stood looking down at his friend, eyes full of pain. "I know what you've tried to do for me, John. No man ever had a better friend. And I'm grateful to have had the opportunity to work with you. But I can't go on." He turned to leave.

Newton hastened after him. "Whatever your own feelings may be, my friend," he said, touching the poet's arm, "my hope for you remains unshaken. The grace of God *is* your good expectation. Now go home and get some rest. And a happy New Year to you. I'll see you tomorrow in church."

Cowper, his hand on the latch, turned and smiled sadly at his friend. The lock clicked softly as he opened the door and disappeared into the night.

* * * * *

Have you ever felt, for one reason or another, as if God was through with you? That you had offended Him one too many times, presumed too much upon His kindness, and cut yourself

69

off from the benefits of His love? If so, there's good news for you in the story of John Newton. Newton knew from experience that the goodness and long-suffering of the Lord are inexhaustible. And having seen this principle demonstrated so often in his own life, he was eager to pass the message of God's never-failing patience along to others who stood in need of a word of encouragement and grace.

If you were even slightly familiar with John Newton before picking up this book, you probably knew him as the author of the enduring and much beloved hymn "Amazing Grace." While Newton filled his life with exploits and adventures of every possible description and went on to become one of the most popular writers and preachers of his day, it is "Amazing Grace" that survives as his most substantial claim to fame.

Even so, the hymn's significance within the larger scheme of Newton's life is not very well understood. Few people realize, for instance, that "Amazing Grace" is just one of more than 280 songs, including "How Sweet the Name of Jesus Sounds" and "Wondrous Things of Thee Are Spoken," that Newton composed during the course of his career. Nor is it common knowledge that, for Newton, hymn writing was simply an extension of a vigorous and highly effective pastoral ministry. Least of all is remembered how powerfully and touchingly these two elements of his legacy—Newton the songwriter and Newton the shepherd of souls—came together within the context of his unique relationship with the poet William Cowper.

Cowper (pronounced *Cooper*), a pre-romantic lyricist whose work earned the respect of such literary luminaries as William Wordsworth and Samuel Taylor Coleridge, came to Olney in 1767 to flee the ghosts of a tortured past. He found refuge in the home of John and Mary Newton. Newton, the former "wretch" and "servant of slaves," had been ordained a minister of the Church of England in 1764, and ever since that time his house had been an "asylum for the perplexed and afflicted."[1] In Cowper's case, this extension of Christian hospitality led to the formation of a close and long-lasting friendship.

"For nearly twelve years," Newton later said of the poet, "we were seldom separated for seven hours at a time when we were awake and at home: the first six I passed daily admiring and aiming to imitate him: during the second six, I walked pensively with him in the valley of the shadow of death."[2]

For "the valley of the shadow of death" was a recurrent theme in Cowper's emotional experience. He was a melancholy character who in our day would almost certainly be diagnosed as bipolar (or manic-depressive). Disappointment in love, professional failure, mental breakdown, attempted suicide—all had played a part in the tragic story of his turbulent life. According to Richard Cecil, "the only sunshine he ever enjoyed" came to him in the form of the eternal assurances he received from the Christian faith.

For more than a decade, John Newton nurtured and encouraged Cowper in that faith. From the beginning of their relationship, the vicar of Olney seemed to possess a keen sensitivity to the special needs of his eccentric and gifted friend. It was largely for therapeutic reasons that Newton invited the poet to assist him in an ongoing project: the composition of hymns designed to supplement the messages of his weekly sermons.

For a time the plan worked well. Cecil tells us that, partly as a result of his collaboration with Newton, Cowper "enjoyed a course of peace for several successive years."[3] So fruitful was their partnership that by the time *The Olney Hymns* were published in 1779 the collection contained more than three hundred selections, sixty-seven of which are attributed to Cowper, including such perennial standards as "Oh! For a Closer Walk with God" and "God Moves in a Mysterious Way."

But hymn writing did not put an end to Cowper's afflictions. Ultimately, his mental and emotional sufferings overwhelmed him in spite of Newton's diligent efforts on his behalf. He broke off the working relationship, inexplicably convinced that he had somehow been excluded from the kingdom of God. "Ask not hymns from a man suffering despair as I do," he wrote. "I could not sing the Lord's song were it to save my life, banished as I am, not to a strange land, but to a remoteness from His presence."[4]

Significantly, this crisis appears to have coincided with the composition of "Amazing Grace." Newton wrote the hymn to accompany a sermon on I Chronicles 17:16-17 and introduced it to his congregation on New Year's Day 1773. It was the last time Cowper ever attended church. By January 2 the poet was deep in the pit of a black depression. And while he continued to write religious poetry and held fast to his Christian convictions for the rest of his life—it was not God but *himself* that he doubted—he never fully recovered from the debilitating effects of this final breakdown.

Was it partly in reaction to Cowper's struggles that Newton wrote his timeless lyric about coming safely through "dangers, toils, and snares"? We can only speculate. But if the poet's story strikes you as a downer—if at this point you're tempted to conclude that grace isn't so amazing after all—it might be worth revisiting the hymn's fifth stanza:

> *Yea, when this flesh and heart shall fail,*
> *And mortal life shall cease,*
> *I shall possess within the veil,*
> *A life of joy and peace.*[5]

Whatever the precise connection between Cowper's situation and the composition of "Amazing Grace," it seems certain that these four lines express the substance of Newton's eternal expectations for his sadly burdened friend. As he said at Cowper's funeral, some twenty-seven years later:

> He [Cowper] suffered much here for twenty-seven years, but eternity is long enough to make amends for all. For what is all he endured in this life, when compared with the rest which remaineth for the children of God?[6]

How could John Newton cast the apparent tragedy of William Cowper's life in such a positive light? The answer is simple: He had tasted the grace of God. He knew from experience that grace is greater than all our sin and deeper than all our despair. He understood that when flesh, heart, and faith fail, God remains faithful, for "He cannot deny Himself" (2 Timothy 2:13). And having tasted this grace, he was quick to apply it to the specifics of his friend's chronic depression, which he interpreted *not* as sin, but as a "physical disorder" and a "constitutional disease."[7] This capacity for long-suffering compassion was to become one of the hallmarks of his ministry.

That in itself is a fact well worth remembering. But it takes on a far greater significance when we remember that

JOHN NEWTON:
Long-Suffering Grace

Newton's gift for pastoral patience and understanding was to surface again in the context of *another* relationship. Where Newton's mentoring failed to bring his desired results in the case of William Cowper, it succeeded brilliantly in the life of William Wilberforce.

LONG-SUFFERING GRACE
Doubt and despair, like death itself, will eventually be swallowed up in grace.

PART II

William Wilberforce

My grace is sufficient for you,
for my power is made perfect
in weakness.

2 Corinthians 12:9, NIV

SUFFICIENT GRACE

"I am the resurrection and the life, saith the Lord."

The words seemed out of place to young William, a mere eight years old, as he watched the lips of a priest greeting his father's casket at the door. Numb with an indifferent grief, William wondered why the opening lines of the service spoke of life when its purpose was to bury the dead.

"He that believeth in me, though he were dead, yet shall he live."

Believe? Did his father believe? Of course, he must have. Would the church have hosted such an elaborate funeral service for a man who rejected God? They must have known what William had observed: that his father had been a good man who led a good life.

"We brought nothing into this world, and it is certain we can carry nothing out."

Robert Wilberforce may have brought nothing into this world, but he had certainly been given a great deal upon arrival. The son of a successful merchant and renowned politician, he proudly traced his ancestry to King Henry II, the twelfth-century English monarch. So, while he may not have been able to bring anything with him to the next world, he did leave much behind for his young heir, William.

"The Lord gave, and the Lord hath taken away; blessed be the name of the Lord."

Blessed? How could they say such a thing at a time like this? Did they really expect William to bless the name of a God who "hath taken away" his daddy—the only source of security, protection, and strength he had ever known? Forty years old is too young for a devoted husband and father to leave this life. Eight years old is too young to understand why God would allow such a thing.

His emotions numb from the shock and flurry of the days since learning of his father's death, William did the best he could to take in the sights and sounds of the liturgy. An occasional phrase penetrated his wandering mind, most notably the priest's reading something from the ninetieth Psalm about the Lord being "our refuge from one generation to another."

If anyone needed a refuge now it would be William's mother, Elizabeth. Losing her husband meant more than an empty bed and aching heart. It would also diminish something she had come to cherish: high society living. Having grown accustomed to the pampered life expected of a prominent merchant-class family, Elizabeth would find it more difficult to engage in lavish forms of entertainment without her beloved companion. The horse races, theatre, balls, and other such activities would lose much of their former appeal by triggering memories of happier days before Robert's death.

Faith would offer little real support. Hers was a religion more of show than substance. Despite a long association with notable Anglican clergy, including a relative who became the Archbishop of Canterbury, Elizabeth never held a strong personal faith, at least not the kind that would uphold her through so great a loss. She embraced religious ritual as part of a well-rounded life—more "Christian ethic" guiding social manners than "Christian redeemer" comforting the afflicted.

As the priest completed his homily from I Corinthians 15, William noticed the time had arrived for those assembled to move graveside. As pallbearers positioned the casket next to

FINDING GOD IN THE STORY OF AMAZING GRACE

the open hole in the ground, the priest and clerks sang in low, joyless tones words that seemed more fitting to the moment.

> *Man that is born of a woman hath but a short*
> *time to live, and is full of misery.*
> *He cometh up, and is cut down, like a flower; . . .*
> *O holy and most merciful Saviour, deliver us not into*
> *the bitter pains of eternal death.*[1]

William felt the wet splash of a tear on his hand. He looked over to see the white of his mother's fingers squeezing his own as the words "bitter pains" released a flood of emotions that, until this moment, had remained carefully guarded. He joined her, wiping his own moist eyes with the other hand while the men lowered his father to his final resting place.

"Forasmuch as it hath pleased Almighty God of His great mercy to take unto Himself the soul of our dear brother Robert Wilberforce here departed, we therefore commit his body to the ground; earth to earth, ashes to ashes, dust to dust."

A few moments later, it was over. Well-wishers filed by William's mother as they left. Some made nice comments about Robert's legacy; most just touched her arm in reassuring support. Few even acknowledged William's presence or his pain. Only the priest's benediction offered any solace to a child stunned by sudden loss: "The grace of our Lord Jesus

* * * * *

Christ, and the love of God and the fellowship of the Holy Ghost, be with us all evermore. Amen."

It seems strange to say that the "grace of our Lord Jesus Christ" was with young William Wilberforce. To take away an eight-year-old boy's father hardly seems an act of kindness. Anyone who has lost a parent during childhood can attest to the lifelong influence of such devastation. Perhaps the loss made William more sympathetic to human suffering than might have otherwise been possible. After all, the common pattern of those who inherit wealth includes the pursuit of personal gratification rather than social concern. In fact, God warned the Israelites of this very tendency as they took possession of the Promised Land.

For the Lord your God is bringing you into a good land, a land of brooks of water, of fountains and springs, that flow out of valleys and hills; a land of wheat and barley, of vines and fig trees and pomegranates, a land of olive oil and honey; a land in which you will eat bread without scarcity, in which you will lack nothing; a land whose stones are iron and out of whose hills you can dig copper. When you have eaten and are full, then you shall bless the Lord your God for the good land which He has given you.

Beware that you do not forget the Lord your God . . . lest—when you have eaten and are full, and have built beautiful houses and dwell in them; and when your herds and your flocks multiply, and your silver

83

and your gold are multiplied, and all that you have is multiplied; when your heart is lifted up, and you forget the Lord your God who brought you out of the land of Egypt, from the house of bondage.

DEUTERONOMY 8:7-14

In this context God commanded His people to diligently teach their children to remember the Lord. They were a generation inheriting great wealth. Sadly, such blessing often unleashes a spirit of self-sufficiency and self-gratification rather than an appropriate concern for those less fortunate. For some reason, living in the lap of luxury tends to make us proud rather than humble, hoarding rather than generous, selfish rather than selfless.

This might have been the story of William Wilberforce had he not experienced the heart-softening cleaver of painful loss. Something in his childhood, possibly his father's untimely death, uniquely tempered this wealthy heir to move beyond self-gratification and social distinction to fill a role few were willing or able to accept.

Several other childhood experiences certainly contributed to Wilberforce's emerging character, including poor eyesight and a sickly disposition. Obstacles and irritations, certainly, but William did not allow either to become an excuse for inactivity. In fact, he was described as mentally and physically energetic. He played sports, suggesting a competitive spirit and force of will that enabled him to overcome hereditary disadvantages. Again, physical limitations hardly seem a good gift from a gracious God. But grace appeared to be invading William's life in ways that, while unwelcome, may have been the very tools required to mold a potentially arrogant socialite into an instrument of divine providence.

William Wilberforce could probably relate to the apostle Paul who, while suffering his own physical challenges, perceived a special grace in the experience of suffering and pain. Paul asked the Lord to remove what he called his "thorn in the flesh" on three separate occasions; God finally answered—but not in the manner Paul had hoped.

And He said to me, "My grace is sufficient for you, for My strength is made perfect in weakness." Therefore most gladly I will rather boast in my infirmities, that the power of Christ may rest upon me. . . . For when I am weak, then I am strong. 2 CORINTHIANS 12:9-10

The death of a father and physical weakness are just two of the tools God used to mold the spirit of this young boy. Left to the natural influences of inherited wealth and prominence, William Wilberforce might very well have become just another self-consumed playboy in British society, blissfully unconcerned about one of the greatest injustices of history.

SUFFICIENT GRACE
Unwelcome pain is often God's perfecting instrument.

And the God of all grace . . .
will himself restore you.

1 PETER 5:10, NIV

INTERVENING GRACE

"They presently saw a town before them, and the name of that town is Vanity; and at the town there is a fair kept, called Vanity Fair."

Young William sat on the edge of his seat, eager to discover how the tale would unfold. Never before had he been so interested in a sermon. Reverend Newton, the famous minister friend of his aunt and uncle, had been visiting their home to deliver a series of messages from John Bunyan's classic book *The Pilgrim's Progress*. Aunt Hannah called the sessions "parlor preaching." William didn't care what they were called. He just wanted to hear the rest of the story.

"Our pilgrims, Christian and Faithful, will pass through Vanity Fair on their way to the Celestial City," explained Reverend Newton. "As must all believers who journey through this life."

William, now ten years old, had recently moved in with his uncle. Having fallen ill shortly after her husband's death, his mother could not take care of him properly. So she sent him to live with Robert's brother and his wife. With no children of their own, they happily took their nephew in to nurture him as the son they might never have. Young William quickly found Reverend Newton's visits to be thoroughly enjoyable.

Parlor sermons, as well as routine visits to the church and chapel, gave William a very different impression of religion than that of the liturgical services he had attended with his parents. Reverend Newton somehow seemed less serious, yet more sincere in his religious devotion. He and the other ministers Mother called "enthusiasts" presented and portrayed a Christianity more to William's liking: one that went beyond the expected ritual, touching the very soul.

"Christian and his companion Faithful intended to walk through the lusty fair without distraction, trying their best to ignore the temptation to purchase vain goods."

Reverend Newton paused, staring deeply into young William's eyes as if the peril described was present with them in that very room. "We must set our hearts with similar determination, mindful of our enemy's tantalizing snares."

Newton continued the story and reflections, somehow making each scene more compelling than the last. William listened as the pilgrims remained resolute, yet found themselves attacked for refusing to buy any of the fair's temporal delights.

And what did the two pilgrims receive for remaining true to their calling? The crowd caged them like carnival freaks before dragging them off for a trial in which three deceptive witnesses—Envy, Superstition, and Pickthank—falsely accused them.

Envy claimed that Faithful had condemned all residents of Vanity by decrying the town's customs as diametrically opposed to Christianity.

Superstition complained that Faithful had called their religion "naught, and such by which a man could by no means please God."

And Pickthank swore that Pilgrim had railed against their "noble prince Beelzebub" and his various friends Lord Carnal Delight, Lord Lechery, Sir Having Greedy, and other community dignitaries.

The accusations angered William's spirit, imbedding in his mind the image of how petty and unjust wicked men can be; a striking contrast to the gracious, patient manner of

Faithful, who refused to compromise truth or righteousness in humble obedience to his Lord.

"Notice the foundation of Faithful's defense," continued Reverend Newton. "He spoke the truth with gentle boldness. But in the end, that truth angered the citizens of Vanity Fair even more. So they killed him. His death, however, was not his demise. As the next scene reveals, a heavenly chariot carried Faithful through the clouds with the sound of a trumpet, bringing him directly to his rightful reward and his true home."

Inviting the small group to join him, Reverend Newton bowed his head and offered up a brief prayer of thanksgiving for gathered friends and the lessons received from the writings of John Bunyan.

After waiting patiently for the adults to express words of thanks and compliments to the beloved minister, young William approached Reverend Newton. A smile formed across the former ship captain's weathered face. With a slight wink of the eye, he waved William into the adjoining room to resume the unfinished chess game carefully preserved since his last visit.

*   *   *   *   *

The death of Robert Wilberforce and subsequent illness of William's mother led to an undoubtedly heart-wrenching decision. He had to be sent away to live with relatives, something no child wants, especially amid such unsettling circumstances as losing one parent and fearing the death of the other. As unwelcome as they may have been at the time, however, the changes forced upon ten-year-old William would prove to be the clear intervention of God in his life, bringing about sympathies and relationships that would profoundly influence his future beliefs and choices.

Like a tiny sprout rescued from a rocky path and replanted in rich, moist soil, William Wilberforce spent two of his most impressionable childhood years with those who modeled a faith experience very different from the one his parents would have instilled.

The most direct influences were, of course, his Uncle William (Robert's brother) and Aunt Hannah. Both had converted to the relatively new evangelical movement.

They had met and befriended John Newton in 1764, five years before their nephew moved in. By 1769 it had become customary for William's uncle and aunt to attend services at John Newton's parish in Olney while on holiday, and for Reverend Newton to visit the Wilberforce home to enjoy the company of friends and present his famous "parlor preaching" on such classic works as *The Pilgrim's Progress*.

Another significant model for William was his Aunt

Hannah's half brother John Thornton. Thornton had converted to Christianity under the preaching of the famous Methodist minister George Whitefield, a pioneer in the growing evangelical movement. One of the wealthiest men in Europe, Thornton adopted a simple lifestyle and invested much of his vast resources into various charitable endeavors, most notably the ministries of preachers like Whitefield. After reading John Newton's biography, Thornton became a significant contributor to Newton's preaching and writing endeavors, eventually giving the modern equivalent of about $120,000 to his work.

Through John Thornton's life, young William saw firsthand how to invest God-given wealth into Christian work. But Thornton went one step further. On at least one occasion, he gave William a large sum of money as a gift with one stipulation—that "some should be given to the poor."[1] As we will discover, the benevolence of John Thornton became an important model for William's later life.

Perhaps the most influential figure in young William's developing faith, however, was John Newton himself. The two forged a close relationship during the period of time William lived with his aunt and uncle. Later, Wilberforce wrote that he loved and valued Newton "as a parent" during his childhood years. Newton, having no children of his own, also came to see the boy as a kind of son.[2] Such touching descriptions suggest an abiding admiration between a hurting boy and his spiritual hero.

After recovering from her illness, William's mother became greatly alarmed when she discovered just how heavily her son had been influenced by John Newton and others she called "enthusiasts." Like many of her day, she despised the evangelical movement, perceiving its followers as people who succumbed to "uncontrollable passions." She wanted her son to have no part of such a poisonous religious culture, so she removed him from his aunt and uncle's home. Elizabeth Wilberforce did everything she could to wash any residue of evangelicalism from William's heart and mind. She wanted him to view men like John Newton as a major social drawback to the upper classes of the day.

But not even his mother could disparage the evangelical minister in the eyes of young William. After all, he had had firsthand experience of Newton's authentic, personal faith. Through their relationship, Wilberforce came to know the heart of evangelical Christianity, falling in love with its rich spiritual soil.

"My religious impressions continued for some time after my return to Hull," Wilberforce later wrote, "but no pains were spared . . . to stifle them, by taking me a great deal into company and to places of amusement. I might almost venture to say that no pious parent ever laboured more to impress a beloved child with sentiments of religion than [was done] to give me a taste for the world and its diversions."[3]

Like the sellers of vain pursuits from Bunyan's tale, Wilberforce's own mother placed worldly diversions before her son, hoping to undermine a religious passion she found distasteful. She even stopped taking him to her own church for fear any spiritual emphasis would reignite his evangelical leanings. Her efforts eventually proved effective, at least in the short term, when William abandoned his blossoming faith during his adolescent years.

One must wonder what might have occurred had God not planted young William among such nurturing influences as his relatives, John Newton, and John Thornton. It seems unlikely he would have ever embraced an evangelical brand of faith. Left at home, Wilberforce might have known only the cold, dead religious ritual found in his mother's form of Christianity. In fact, he later compared the upper class's attitude toward converts to evangelicalism as comparable to the way Jews had been "hated" in *Ivanhoe*.[4] It was a hatred he might have adopted himself if not for the intervening grace of a God who intended to ignite Wilberforce's own enthusiasm in order to motivate opposition to the petty, unjust ways of wicked men.

"But may the God of all grace, who called us to His eternal glory by Christ Jesus, after you have suffered a while, perfect, establish, strengthen, and settle you" (I Peter 5:10).

INTERVENING GRACE

God intervenes in human affairs to fulfill His purposes.

As iron sharpens iron, so one man sharpens another.

<small>PROVERBS 27:17, NIV</small>

GIFTING GRACE

Tempers flared as members of the House of Commons argued over what to do about the disastrous war with the Americans. With the French supporting the former colonies and the Dutch sending supplies to the rebels, the British government saw little point in continuing a fight that seemed destined to fail. Watching the debate from the House gallery, twenty-one-year-old William Wilberforce found himself agreeing with those calling for peace.

"May I join you?" The voice sounded familiar. Turning to look, William recognized a former St. John's College classmate. The two had been acquaintances, though never friends as each ran in different circles.

"Certainly. William Wilberforce at your service."

"Yes, I remember. We endured mathematics under the same tutor as I recall. Pitt, William Pitt, at your service, sir." Wilberforce moved his book to make room for the welcome company.

"May I ask your opinion on the matter under discussion?" Always the diplomat, Pitt's question betrayed nothing of his own leanings.

"I side with those advocating an end to the war."

Pitt's smile and nod suggested a kindred spirit.

"I hope to argue the same if I am given the honor." The comment did not surprise Wilberforce. Even his colleagues at St. John's assumed the younger Pitt would enter political life following the footsteps of his famous father. With such a keen intellect and calm disposition, William Pitt seemed perfectly suited for a seat in Parliament.

Wilberforce had recently become interested in politics himself. The wealth inherited from his family placed him in the enviable position of selecting between several possible life pursuits. William could have dedicated himself to business like his father, but Cousin Abel Smith handled the money so effectively it seemed pointless to interfere. He might have chosen the life of pleasure—something he had tasted during his playful college years. But the experience had left him unsatisfied. His ambition hungered for more than social pretense and card parties.

WILLIAM WILBERFORCE:
Gifting Grace

Wilberforce may not have had the temperament or stature of a William Pitt, but he possessed more of the means and skills necessary for public office than many he had observed in action while watching from his gallery bench. In addition to his money, a necessity to such pursuits, he had many talents that might lend themselves to political life, including a winning personality and social grace that put others at ease. In childhood, William's teacher had often placed him upon a classroom table to read aloud as an example of eloquence to the other boys.[1] He also had a knack for writing, evidenced by his first published composition at the age of fourteen: a letter to the editor of the *Yorkshire Gazette* condemning slavery.[2]

"Wouldn't it be something to speak with eloquence and conviction as Fox spoke yesterday?" Knowing himself a natural orator, Wilberforce considered Charles James Fox and his opposition colleagues an inspiration to his own aspirations. "I've been pondering public service myself." William's voice betrayed an uncertainty and insecurity at the prospect of pursuing such a lofty aim.

"Would you care to dine with me during the next recess?" asked Pitt. "I would like to hear more of your intentions, and discover what other interests we might share."

After their meal, Wilberforce and Pitt returned to their seats in the House of Commons gallery to observe the proceedings. They had discovered much in common while enjoying their meal. William's faint inkling toward political life found a source of encouragement, and he had a strong sense that the chance reacquaintance of two former Cambridge classmates might just be the start of an important, lifelong friendship.

* * * * *

By the time seventeen-year-old William Wilberforce left his home in 1776 to attend St. John's College at Cambridge, his future was secure. He had inherited a great fortune, which enabled him to live a life of privilege. Since her son was long removed from the influence of his aunt and uncle, William's mother had managed to pamper her son into viewing diligence and sacrifice as the unfortunate domain of those who must earn their own way in life. A naturally talented, wealthy young man like William, on the other hand, should not have to worry about stringent academic rigor. Like his mother, he could coast into becoming a person of standing who did little more than enjoy the good life.

It didn't take long for William to begin wasting his time and opportunity. As he later recalled, "I was introduced, on the very first night of my arrival, to as licentious a set of men as can well be conceived. They drank hard, and their conversation was even worse than their lives. I lived amongst them for some time . . . often indeed I was horror-struck at their conduct—and after the first year I shook off in a great measure my connection with them."[3]

Thankfully, William had enough maturity to resist the pull into debauchery, finding more promising friends. But he continued to waste his time and talents. Even those responsible to guide his academic success fed the notion that privilege exempts one from hard work.

"Their object seemed to be, to make and keep me idle," explained Wilberforce. "If ever I appeared studious, they would say to me: 'Why in the world should a man of your fortune trouble yourself?' Whilst my companions were reading hard and attending lectures, card parties and idle amusements consumed my time. The tutors would often say within my hearing, that 'they were mere saps, but that [Wilberforce] did all by talent.' This was poison to a mind constituted like mine."[4]

Later in life, Wilberforce would repent that he had wasted so much of his time and potential during his college years. At the time, however, it made him one of the more popular young men on campus. "There was no one at all like him for powers of entertainment," wrote dormmate Thomas Gisborne. "[He was] always fond of repartee and discussion. . . . There was always a great Yorkshire pie in his rooms, and all were welcome to partake of it."[5] Gisborne recalled several occasions in which late in the evening after long hours of diligent study he would hear Wilberforce's melodious voice in the next room inviting him to come and sit to chat before going to bed, a dangerous invitation for one trying to remain focused on his academic duties.

According to Wilberforce biographer Kevin Belmonte, such stories paint a picture of a young man who was popular because he used his wealth "to grease the skids toward social prominence. There was a real possibility of his taking the wrong fork in the road and wasting his life—becoming an indolent, self-absorbed person."[6]

Across the Cambridge campus, another wealthy young man followed a very different path. William Pitt, far more serious and intellectually oriented than Wilberforce, threw himself into his studies with an eye toward a political career after graduation. "I was acquainted with Mr. Pitt at Cambridge," recalls Wilberforce "but we were not at that time [close]. He, indeed, lived in a higher set than myself; but in the winter after we had each left college I often met him in the gallery of the House of Commons, which we were both fond of attending."[7]

One of the most beautiful expressions of God's grace is His compulsion to rescue us from our own folly, remolding our messes into something He can use to accomplish His greater purposes. In the case of Wilberforce, rescue came in the form of an unlikely friendship. Having previously run in very different circles while on divergent life paths, Wilberforce and Pitt now forged a friendship that motivated William to turn away from vain pursuits and toward a career he had only hesitantly considered. This career, incidentally, would ultimately require the kind of hard work and self-sacrifice he had spent his college years avoiding at all costs.

For twenty-five years, until Pitt's death in 1806, Wilberforce would benefit from the example and support of the man he considered a true friend and partner in the battle to end slavery.

William Wilberforce had been given many gifts, including tremendous wealth, natural eloquence, and social charm. But they might have all gone to waste if not for another gift: the blessing of friendship. "As iron sharpens iron, so one man sharpens another," wrote Solomon. The men in William's life during his college years had had a dulling effect. Pitt, on the other hand, became the first of many future leaders to sharpen Wilberforce through the inspiration of common vision, complementary talents, and the motivation needed to move beyond a destiny of pleasure to one of greatness.

GIFTING GRACE

One of the greatest gifts in life is a good friend.

If anyone is in Christ, he is a new creation; old things have passed away; behold, all things have become new.

2 CORINTHIANS 5:17

CHANGING GRACE

William's twenty-five-year-old body was sore from the incessant bumps and jolts that defined a long winter journey. Fortunately, the conversation kept him entertained, or at least challenged, as the carriage rode across the snow-packed ground.

"Hits the nail on the head, doesn't it, Wilber?" asked his traveling companion. A large, forceful man, Isaac Milner was accustomed to winning arguments—something William had observed as a lad when Milner served as his tutor. Only nine years older than Wilberforce, Milner had since been named chairman of natural philosophy at Cambridge University. Their paths had crossed again during William's recent visit to Scarborough. Enjoying Milner's good nature and entertaining manner, William had invited Isaac to join him on his holiday trip.

"I think Doddridge had someone like you in mind when he penned those words!" The smile in Milner's voice gave William cause to reread the passage.

> You own that there is a God, and well you may, for you cannot open your eyes but you must see the evident proofs of his being, his presence, and his agency. You behold him around you in every object. You feel him within you, if I may so speak, in every vein and in every nerve. You see and you feel not only that he hath formed you with an exquisite wisdom which no mortal man could ever fully explain or comprehend, but that he is continually near you, wherever you are, and however you are employed, by day or by night; "in him [you] live, and move, and have [your] being." (see Acts 17:28)

Published forty years earlier, *On the Rise and Progress of Religion in the Soul* was written by Philip Doddridge. The book had been lying on a table in the room Isaac had been staying in while on holiday. William picked it up and began thumbing through its pages before asking his traveling companion what he thought of the book. "It is one of the best books ever written," Milner replied. "Let's take it with us and read it on our journey."[1] So they did.

William wondered why Milner would connect Doddridge's words to him. He certainly couldn't argue the point. He acknowledged God's existence and possessed an intuitive knowledge of His sustaining presence. But it had been years since William held the beliefs he had adopted while living with his aunt and uncle. Lately, he found himself more comfortable with the God presented by Reverend Lindsey at the Unitarian Chapel: a benign Providence who expected proper living—but little more. Belief in Christ's divinity, the Christian doctrine of atonement, and the authority of Scripture no longer fit William's theological comfort zone.

That is why Wilberforce found it surprising that Doddridge's words seemed to resonate so—a well-reasoned, elegant explanation of Christianity. Doddridge's writings were popular in polite society, yet his perspective was remarkably similar to the despised and oft slandered "enthusiasts."

Even if Wilberforce wanted to ignore the book's message, he couldn't, thanks to Isaac Milner, a man who seemed determined to make sure William confronted each and every point; including several far more confrontational than the existence of a generic awareness of the Almighty:

> I beseech you, reader, whoever you are, that you would now look seriously into your own heart, and ask it this one plain question; Am I truly religious? Is the love of God the governing principle of my life? Do I walk under the sense of his presence? Do I converse with him from day to day, in the exercise of prayer and praise? And am I, on the whole, making his service my business and my delight, regarding him as my master and my father?

Asking himself such questions proved unsettling for William; he knew he was somewhat apathetic when it came to religious concerns. Put simply, no—loving God was not the governing principle of his life.

> Do you not in your conscience believe there will be a future judgment? Do you not believe there is an invisible and eternal world? . . . Must you not sooner or later be brought to think of these things, whether you wilt or not! And in the mean time do you not certainly know that timely and serious reflection upon them is, through divine grace, the only way to prevent your ruin! Yes, sinner, I need not multiply words on a subject like this. Your conscience is already inwardly convinced, though your pride may be unwilling to own it.[2]

WILLIAM WILBERFORCE:
Changing Grace

The further they read together, the more William saw himself exposed. One by one, Doddridge undercut the various excuses, objections, and obstacles that prevented William from acknowledging his need, and presented the solution offered through the grace of Jesus Christ. Something had begun within him that could not easily be dismissed.

"So Wilber," came the voice of his former academic tutor turned spiritual mentor, "what will you do?"

* * * * *

He called it "The Great Change." It didn't happen all at once, but rather gradually as Wilberforce seriously examined and began to accept orthodox Christianity after years of being skeptical of its more demanding claims. Two "chance" encounters converged to carry William where he might otherwise have never gone: into direct confrontation with the God behind evangelical passion.

The first encounter was a renewed relationship with Isaac Milner. Enjoying one another's company over a game of cards in some Scarborough pub, Wilberforce did not perceive the fun-loving Milner to be any more religiously devout than himself. Had he known just how seriously Milner took his Christian faith, in fact, William would not have extended the invitation to join him on holiday. "Had I known at first what his opinions were," wrote Wilberforce, "it would have decided me against making him the offer." But he did make the offer, an act he later attributed to God's grace. "A gracious hand leads us in ways that we know not, and blesses us not only without, but even against, our plans and inclinations."[3]

The second encounter occurred when Wilberforce happened across the book by Doddridge. Any other writer could well have pushed William further away rather than draw him closer to a personal understanding of faith. After all, he had by this time embraced a perspective much closer to that of his mother, one that considered "enthusiasm" lacking in critical thought about spiritual realities. As biographer Kevin Belmonte explains, Wilberforce "had been raised in polite society" and his temperament was "ill suited to anything that might have been written in [a]dour, pedantic tone."[4] *On the Rise and Progress of Religion in the Soul* was the ideal book for him.

Between Philip Doddridge's compelling prose and Isaac Milner's winsome manner, William Wilberforce came face-to-face with a Christianity far more intellectually satisfying and emotionally moving than he had previously encountered. The time spent riding across the continent in that carriage had a dramatic impact on Wilberforce, launching an irreversible quest toward a deeper understanding of the faith.

Duties in Parliament interrupted the quest for several months as Wilberforce responded to the urgent demands of his close friend, Prime Minister William Pitt. But in June 1785

WILLIAM WILBERFORCE:
Changing Grace

Isaac and Wilberforce picked up their conversation where it had left off when they traveled together to the Swiss Alps. This time, they read the New Testament together in the original language. William raised questions and doubts and Milner responded to each, offering insight and deeper understanding of the Scripture to his young protégé. By the end of their journey, Wilberforce recalls having achieved "a settled conviction in my mind, not only of the truth of Christianity, but also of the scriptural basis of the leading doctrines which I now hold."[5]

Wilberforce did not tell anyone at first. Knowing few other religiously devout people, he decided to confide in his childhood father figure, Reverend John Newton. The news had to be handled privately since word of their renewed friendship would certainly have harmed Wilberforce's political influence and social standing. He sent a sealed letter to Newton at his church requesting a secret meeting to discuss "ten thousand doubts within myself." He also requested confidentiality "till I release you from the obligation."

Newton did meet with Wilberforce, eager to see how God had answered the minister's prayers for William to regain a desire for the faith he had tasted in childhood. Offering much needed encouragement and counsel, Newton once again played a vital role as an instrument of God's changing grace in Wilberforce's life.

Before long, William's religious confidence increased. His was indeed a "great change." He became, in the words of Paul, "a new creation; old things have passed away; behold, all things have become new" (2 Corinthians 5:17).

Within a few months' time, however, Wilberforce found himself troubled by the implications his conversion carried with it. He knew that such beliefs required one to act upon them, not merely give vague intellectual assent. "My anguish of soul for some months was indescribable," he later recalled.[6]

Wilberforce's evangelical perspective became the driving force behind his desire to end slavery and invest in many philanthropic efforts in order to alleviate suffering among the poor. This was not surprising since the first chapter of Philip Doddridge's book described such benevolence as the proper affect of sincere Christian belief.

> He is a barbarian, and deserves not to be called a man, who can look upon the sorrows of his fellow creatures without drawing out his soul unto them and wishing, at least, that it were in the power of his hand to help them.[7]

CHANGING GRACE
Friends can be tools in the workshop of
God's changing grace.

Let each one remain with God in that state in which he was called.

1 CORINTHIANS 7:24

CALLING GRACE

The moment he entered the room, Pitt could tell something had changed in his friend's countenance. This was a different Wilberforce than he had known; a man more lamb than lion, more pensive than proud. Pitt had hoped William's letter suggesting withdrawal from public life had been a momentary lapse in judgment, simply a reaction to stress or discouragement. The look in Wilber's eyes told him otherwise.

"It is good to see you again my friend." Pitt embraced the man who had become more brother than colleague.

"Thank you for coming, William," Wilberforce responded, lifting a page he had placed beside him on the desk. "I can't tell you how much your letter meant to me. I'm not sure I would have been so gracious in your place."

"Well, I must confess that I required a brief cooling down period before I could properly respond." The grin on Pitt's face assured William that their friendship had survived the revelation. "But I respect the courage and character sending that letter required of you."

"Then you understand my decision?"

"I didn't say that," Pitt responded, taking a seat beside William. "You and I have much to discuss, starting with this 'great change' of yours."

For the next few hours the two talked; Wilberforce telling of his friendship with Isaac Milner, reading passages from Doddridge's book, and describing his gradual but certain conversion from a religion of social pretense to a faith that encompassed all of life—including one's profession.

"I know how much you have depended upon me to fight the battles necessary to your agenda." William's voice seemed an odd mix of deep conviction and hesitant excuse making. "Despite my love for you as a friend and respect for you in Parliament, I can no longer be as loyal a party man." Both knew what he meant. Wilberforce had earned a reputation as Pitt's "pit bull" whenever it became necessary to destroy a political opponent; his elocution was a weapon few could survive.

"Contrary to the common perception," William continued, "religion should effect more than inward feelings. It requires a change in one's very disposition and conduct."

WILLIAM WILBERFORCE:
Calling Grace

Others sensed a change in Wilberforce's disposition, one friend even sending a letter to his mother concerned that a "melancholy madness" had overtaken his once bold temperament. His formerly ambitious character seemed to have been dampened, causing some to fear he had lost—rather than come to—his senses during his "great change."

Being as skeptical as Wilberforce had been before his conversion, Pitt tried to reason his friend out of his enthusiast convictions. He quickly discovered William's change to have a solid intellectual foundation. So he chose a different approach: appealing to—rather than undermining—the teachings of Christianity.

"William, I simply can't see you living the contemplative life. Certainly religion calls some to active engagement rather than passive reflection!" Pitt's confidence grew as he sensed Wilberforce being receptive to his argument. "Surely the principles as well as the practice of Christianity lead not to meditation only but to action."[1]

Indeed, the active life would be a legitimate calling for Wilberforce. But not the kind he had pursued thus far. His pursuit of influence and distinction, the "darling object" of his life, had made him more of a political animal than he now cared to admit. Like many who achieve success at so early an age, Wilberforce had succumbed to the many temptations of ambition.

"I am taking some time to reflect," William explained to Pitt while walking him to the door. "I promise to seriously consider your wise counsel."

"Remember my friend," said Pitt as he turned back from his waiting carriage, "you have much to offer in public life. I beg of you, think of the good that can be done."

As he closed the door and returned to his study, William realized this decision would be much harder than he had assumed. He needed more time and more counsel.

* * * * *

Os Guinness calls it the "Eusebian temptation," a belief that to serve God best one must enter a sacred rather than a secular occupation. Shortly after his conversion to evangelical Christianity, William Wilberforce seriously contemplated leaving the secular work of politics in order to devote himself fully to some sort of sacred work in ministry. By God's grace, however, he held off a decision until after reflecting for a season upon what Scripture taught and others thought.

Having begun to see his life as one of selfish ambition and wasted potential, Wilberforce thought a return to politics might somehow be inconsistent with his new faith. One can imagine the crisis of confidence this must have created in a man accustomed to pursuing his dreams with little regard for

God's opinion on the matter. In order to determine his next step, William began spending several hours a day in Bible study and in self-examination. During this period he copied a line from Sir Francis Bacon's *Essays*: "It is a sad fate for a man to die too well known to everybody else, and still unknown to himself."[2] Wilberforce knew he couldn't bear the prospect of being occupied with duties that would lead to worldly fame while never knowing the part God had intended for his life.

During this season of reflection, Jesus' words became a splinter in Wilberforce's heart. "Thou shalt love the Lord thy God with all thy heart, and with all thy soul, and with all thy strength, and with all thy mind; and thy neighbour as thyself" (Luke 10:27, KJV). Taking his cue from the story of the Good Samaritan, William concluded that in order to fulfill the command he must "consider our peculiar situations, and in these to do all the good we can."[3]

He spent the winter of 1786 living near St. Mary Woolnoth Church in order to seek pastoral counsel from its rector, Reverend John Newton. Knowing how his association with such a famous "enthusiast" would appear, Wilberforce tried to meet with Newton in confidence. But his intentions were thwarted when a friend saw the two of them walking together—inciting rumors to the world (and William's mother) that Wilberforce had become one of those despised

Methodists. "May God grant it may be said with truth,"[4] he wrote in his diary, suggesting diminishing concern over personal reputation.

We can imagine Newton and Wilberforce discussing the matter of calling. How do we know in which section of the vineyard the Lord would have us work? Is it wise to withdraw from the corrupting influences and vanity of worldly pursuits in order to dedicate oneself fully to God? Many in the emerging evangelical movement, including Newton himself, felt compelled to leave secular careers for full-time ministry. Should William do the same?

Certainly, Newton and Wilberforce discussed the writings of the apostle Paul, such as his admonition to the church at Corinth:

Let every man abide in the same calling wherein he was called. . . . For he that is called in the Lord, being a servant, is the Lord's freeman: likewise also he that is called, being free, is Christ's servant. Ye are bought with a price; be not ye the servants of men. Brethren, let every man, wherein he is called, therein abide with God.

1 CORINTHIANS 7:20, 22-24, KJV

Since Wilberforce had been called by Christ while in public service, did that mean he should "abide with God" in that calling?

Such conversations between Wilberforce and Newton became a turning point for William as he attempted to make one of the most important decisions of his life. While we can only speculate on the specifics, we know that Newton encouraged William to view public life as the place he might do "all the good" possible. Ten years later, when Wilberforce again faced a similar career decision, Newton reinforced the advice given during their 1786 chats.

> You meet with many things which weary and disgust you . . . they are inseparably connected with your path of duty; and though you cannot do all the good you wish for, some good is done. . . . It costs you something . . . and exposes you to many impertinences from which you would gladly be exempted; but if, upon the whole, you are thereby instrumental in promoting the cause of God and the public good, you will have no reason [for] regret. . . . Nor is it possible at present to calculate all the advantages that may result from your having a seat in the House at such a time as this. . . . You are not only a representative for Yorkshire, you have the far greater honour of being a representative for the Lord, in a place where many know Him not, and an opportunity of showing them what are the genuine fruits of that religion which you are known to profess. . . .

Indeed the great point for our comfort in life is to have a well-grounded persuasion that we are, where, all things considered, we ought to be. Then it is no great matter whether we are in public or in private life, in a city or a village, in a palace or a cottage.[5]

Shortly after his time with Newton, Wilberforce wrote a letter to his mother reassuring her that he would not, as she feared, become a recluse. He had chosen to remain "where Providence has placed me."[6] William made the decision to fulfill the calling of God to "love thy neighbor as thyself" by using his influence in Parliament.

CALLING GRACE
The call of God makes secular duties a sacred vocation.

> *"Who knows whether you have
> come to the kingdom for such a
> time as this?"*
>
> ESTHER 4:14

DISTURBING GRACE

"So, you've been meeting with Thomas Clarkson?" Pitt's question sounded more like an announcement than inquiry.

"Yes, for several months now," Wilberforce responded as he felt the grass for a dry spot to sit. "Did you know that he wrote a prize-winning Latin essay about the slave trade when he was studying at Cambridge? He called on me to help him research the subject shortly after my meeting with Middleton."

Pitt glanced at his cousin, William Grenville, as he pulled

a dead branch from the oak tree under which the three had decided to let their meal digest. Noticing the nonverbal exchanges between Pitt and Grenville suggested an agenda, Wilberforce began to suspect this was more than a social gathering.

"Isn't it a bit risky for a rising member of Parliament to be seen consorting with the likes of Clarkson and Middleton?" asked Grenville. "Rumor has it they are conspiring to form some sort of committee opposing the slave trade."

"Yes, it's called the Committee for the Abolition of the Slave Trade. They signed a charter this year. In fact, that's why Middleton approached me." Wilberforce suspected the two already knew that. "They need someone to champion their cause in Parliament."

"Any particular someone?" Pitt inquired.

"Well, they hoped I might consider the opportunity." William tried to maintain an impartial tone to avoid revealing his interest. After all, Pitt was trying to keep his party unified, and nothing would split it faster than one of his close allies putting forth an abolitionist proposal. If Wilberforce ever hoped to enter the fray, however, he knew the prime minister's approval would be essential.

"Not long ago you shocked me by announcing you might abandon public life for religious contemplation. Are you now considering a cause that is sure to create division in the ranks?"

Pitt prodded further, feeding William's growing apprehension. "Wilber, you know that the only thing less popular than an enthusiast is an abolitionist enthusiast!"

"I realize that." William leaned his head back against the large trunk, taking in the rustling sound and much needed refreshment of the springtime breeze. "And I know the history. The Quakers repeatedly failed to gain any momentum against the commercial and shipping interests. What's more, you know that anyone who takes up this cause will be accused of trying to undermine the economic foundation of our empire."

Grenville and Pitt said nothing, waiting for Wilberforce to reveal his intentions.

"But I'm increasingly convinced that I should oppose what is without question an intolerable evil." William stood and paced as he spoke—his usual posture when making an argument in the House. "Do you remember me telling you about my meeting with James Ramsay, the Scottish minister who witnessed the horrors of slavery firsthand? His essay has since been published. To read it ignites an irrepressible desire to do something. His own church boycotted him for trying to convert slaves to Christianity. If men like him can withstand such abuse, what excuse have I?"

"You seem resolved then." Pitt forced William's hand. "Have you accepted Middleton's offer to become champion of their cause?"

"No, I haven't. But I cannot shake off the desire. It is almost as if God Himself were handing me the task. How does one ignore such a prompting?"

"One does not, my dear friend," Pitt responded reassuringly. "You accept the challenge and lead the cause!" Surprised by such a comment, William's eyes darted to the prime minister's face.

"Forgive my scheming, Wilber," Pitt continued, "but I, too, have spoken with Middleton and Clarkson. In fact, Grenville and I invited you here today hoping to convince you of the conclusion you have already reached. Thankfully, it appears you need little urging on our part."

After putting the puzzle pieces together in his mind, William allowed a big smile of relief to spread across his face. The three had a good laugh at the irony of the moment. But the enormity and peril of the task quickly settled over them. Wilberforce looked out in contemplation upon the horizon as Grenville broke the silence.

"We can think of no one better suited to lead the effort, William."

"More than that," added Pitt, "I believe this may be the one cause big enough to keep you from doing something as crazy as leaving my party to become an obscure, Methodist minister!"

"Then you approve?" an excited William asked his friend and leader.

WILLIAM WILBERFORCE:
Disturbing Grace

"Why don't you give notice of a motion on the subject of the slave trade? You've taken great pains to collect the evidence, and you possess the talents and character needed for such a significant task."

As they walked together back toward the house, all three men knew that William Wilberforce would soon become a champion of the floundering abolitionist movement.

* * * * *

"God Almighty," Wilberforce wrote in his journal shortly after a pivotal meeting with Sir Charles Middleton, "has set before me two great objects, the suppression of the slave trade and the reformation of manners." It is unlikely the first of these "objects" would have occurred had it not been for the work and influence of several who had gone before. We all stand on the shoulders of heroes. In the case of Wilberforce, those heroes include relatively unknown men and women who campaigned long and hard against slavery—many of whom never lived to see its demise.

James Ramsay, for example, first encountered the horrors of the slave trade fifteen years before meeting Wilberforce. While serving as a surgeon aboard the royal navy ship *Arundel*, Ramsay was ordered by his captain to inspect a ship carrying slaves. The foul stench of human feces and vomit invaded his nostrils as Ramsay observed African men and women tightly packed into the hull, gasping for air. Having contracted the plague, they desperately needed whatever help Ramsay could provide. After doing what little he could to ease the suffering of the poor men and women on that ship, Ramsay returned to the *Arundel* determined to do something to end the dreadful practice.

Ramsay later became an Anglican minister on a Caribbean island near large sugar plantations. His parishioners objected when he began opening the church doors to blacks in hopes of converting the slaves to Christianity. They boycotted his church when he began to criticize planters for their cruel treatment of the slaves. Reverend Ramsay returned to Britain under pressure and spent three years writing the *Essay on the Treatment and Conversion of African Slaves in the British Sugar Colonies.* The essay was published in 1784, shortly after a conversation between the minister and William Wilberforce.

Up until Ramsay's book was published, antislavery writings had very little impact, as they were often disregarded as the work of zealously sanctimonious Quakers or Methodists. Partly due to his credibility as an eyewitness and a mainstream Anglican writer, Ramsay's *Essay* had tremendous influence. In fact, a substantial portion of the slavery debate in the latter half of the 1780s centered on his work, and many—Wilberforce included—modeled their own approach to the issue after Ramsay.[1]

WILLIAM WILBERFORCE:
Disturbing Grace

But Ramsay, like most religious leaders who condemned slavery from their pulpits and pens, could not defeat the powerful forces defending the system. This was something his friend and former sea captain, Sir Charles Middleton, understood when he and others formed the Committee for the Abolition of the Slave Trade in 1787. They needed someone who shared their hatred of slavery, someone who shared their Christian convictions, and someone with the political platform to influence the highest echelons of society.

As luck would have it, a young politician who had recently embraced evangelical Christianity just happened to be looking for a way to "do all the good possible." William Wilberforce had been counseled to remain in Parliament because it was where Providence had placed him, although he did not yet know how his faith would inform that mandate. Wilberforce had the right gifts and the right heart at the right time for the task. The only thing he needed was a few strategic nudges.

The first nudge was the influence of abolitionist enthusiasts like Ramsay, Middleton, Clarkson, and others. The second was a period of disturbing research into the subject, which solidified his earlier inclination to oppose such an inhumane system. The third included a changed heart, making him eager to use his office for something more important than personal prestige—and willing to risk his reputation for a greater good. Finally, he needed the nudge of William

Pitt's approval to tackle the issue, which he received when Pitt encouraged him to remain in public life.

Consider the story of Queen Esther. Learning about the impending murder of her people, Esther faced a difficult choice: speak up on behalf of the Jews or quietly preserve her own life. Faced with her moment of truth, a frightened young girl listened to the advice of the man who raised her.

"Do not think in your heart that you will escape in the king's palace any more than all the other Jews. For if you remain completely silent at this time, relief and deliverance will arise for the Jews from another place. . . . Yet who knows whether you have come to the kingdom for such a time as this?" ESTHER 4:13-14

Don't miss the significance of this. Mordecai did not advise Esther to intervene because she was the only hope. He knew that the main plot of God's grand drama involved the Jewish people, and he knew that God would prevent their extermination with or without her help. The question was not what would happen in the larger story, but whether Esther would fulfill the part she had been chosen to play.

Wilberforce faced a similar moment. For some reason—perhaps this reason—he had been placed in a position of unique influence. He could choose the path of self-preservation, quietly going about his own business. Or he could enter the dangerous fray of speaking out on behalf of others. Certainly, God could have used someone else to accomplish

His purposes. But He uniquely positioned William Wilberforce with the gifts, passions, status, and relationships necessary to fulfill a significant part in this story of redemption.

DISTURBING GRACE
God often moves us into uncomfortable places in order to accomplish His purpose in our lives.

But as for you, brethren, do not grow weary in doing good.

2 THESSALONIANS 3:13

PERSISTENT GRACE

The stage had been set. William Wilberforce could not have asked for a more ideal set of circumstances to once again advance his cause.

First, he demonstrated good faith with potential enemies by interrupting a subversive plan to defeat the Treason and Sedition bills, placing him in the good graces of many who had accused abolitionists of opposing the Crown. Having achieved this brilliant political move only weeks earlier, Wilberforce returned to London a hero among many who had mistakenly assumed him disloyal.

Second, bringing the slave trade before the House now could snatch the issue away from those calling abolitionists "revolutionaries." The charge had resurfaced when violence erupted among slaves in the British West Indies, causing some to cower in the face of mischaracterization and false accusations. Wilberforce, however, refused to give ground. He boldly leveraged his current political capital to squash the idea that abolition was a fringe, radical movement. "Now is the very time," he announced, "to show our true principles by stopping a practice which violates all the real rights of human nature."[1]

Third, unlike past attempts to advance a bill ending the slave trade, it seemed that this time Wilberforce had enough votes. Momentum had shifted dramatically since his first effort five years earlier when only one third of the House voted with him. It would be close, but the scales appeared to be tipping in the direction of abolition.

So, confident in the likelihood of success, William Wilberforce introduced his motion for a bill to abolish the slave trade on February 2, 1796.

Right away, he lost a key ally. Robert Banks Jenkinson had earlier condemned the slave trade, but then hurt the cause by proposing the question be postponed until "the return of peace." Delay had been the most successful tactic used against Wilberforce from the start, and it did nothing to ease the misery of slavery's victims. William passionately opposed the suggestion.

"There is something not a little provoking in the dry calm way in which gentlemen are apt to speak of the sufferings of others." Wilberforce peered at Jenkinson as if looking at Judas himself. "The question suspended! Is the desolation of wretched Africa suspended? Are all the complicated miseries of this atrocious trade—is the work of death suspended? No, sir, I will not delay this motion, and I call upon the House not to insult the forbearance of Heaven by delaying this tardy act of justice."[2]

Others scoffed, undermining Wilberforce's appeal to compassion by claiming the slaves were well fed.

"What!" came his indignant retort. "Are these the only claims of a rational being? Are the feelings of the heart nothing? . . . So far from thanking the honourable gentleman for the feeding, clothing, and lodging of which he boasts, I protest against the way in which he has mentioned them as degrading men to the level of brutes, and insulting all the higher qualities of our common nature."[3]

With each point, support for abolition grew. Sensing Wilberforce's growing momentum, General Banastre Tarleton motioned for adjournment. Like the rest of William's opponents, he wanted to stop the bleeding caused by such forceful eloquence. But the request was soundly defeated, further assuring Wilberforce that his bill would indeed go forward.

A few weeks later, on February 22, the bill's first reading faced no opposition, allowing it to move toward a second reading on the evening of March 3. In a last-minute maneuver by a slave-trade supporter, however, the reading was moved to an earlier part of the day before Wilberforce and his allies planned to attend. Learning of the change, William quickly ran to the House and began speaking until the others showed up. They arrived in time to carry the bill (63 to 31), placing it in committee where it passed by a three-quarters margin. The bill to end the slave trade made it all the way to its third reading with no serious opposition beyond a few attempts to delay or subvert the process.

William's political instinct had been right, and success was within reach, which made what happened next a bitter pill to swallow.

On March 15, the bill fell to defeat by a mere four votes. "Ten or twelve of those who had supported me were absent," William later wrote in his journal. Using one last dirty trick, supporters of the slave trade had given free opera tickets to select members of the House. Had those few been in attendance rather than attending the theatre, the bill would have carried. It would be eleven years before William Wilberforce would again come so close to victory.

WILLIAM WILBERFORCE:
Persistent Grace

Days later, overwhelmed by feelings of grief and betrayal, Wilberforce became seriously ill.

* * * * *

"Hope deferred makes the heart sick" (Proverbs 13:12). Throughout 1796, William Wilberforce knew exactly what Solomon meant when he penned those words. Near victory followed by sudden defeat threw William into his darkest days, including a physical and emotional collapse that some have described as a nervous breakdown. He even considered withdrawing entirely from public life because the thought of resuming the cause triggered feelings of "terror."

What a contrast from the confident demeanor of the young Wilberforce, who had entered political life fifteen years earlier to advance his own social standing. That young man could not have anticipated that he would one day feel worn out and beaten down from his efforts to advance the freedom of others. But a "great change" shoved William beyond safe, popular causes into the deep water of the most heated political battle of his generation.

It would be difficult to fault Wilberforce for throwing in the towel. After all, he had been accused of "enthusiast" inspirations, revolutionary aspirations, and self-righteous inclinations. He had the thankless task of leading a cause considered by many to be the domain of evangelical preachers trying to force religious piety down the throats of sophisticated society. His reputation had been thrashed, his life threatened, his health spent, and now his efforts thwarted by those defending their own bank accounts by destroying human dignity. How, he must have wondered, could he go on suffering while they went on smiling?

The answer came from John Newton in response to a letter Wilberforce penned in July 1796, just a few months after his bill's defeat. Hoping his mentor would agree that it was time for him to retire from public life, William received another charge to stay the course.

> Some of God's people may be emphatically said not to live to themselves. May it not be said of you? . . . You meet with many things which weary and disgust you . . . but then they are inseparably connected with your path of duty. . . .
>
> Though you have not, as yet, fully succeeded in your persevering endeavors to abolish the slave trade, the business is still in [process]; and since you took it in hand, the condition of the slaves in our islands, has undoubtedly been already [improved] . . . You have not labored in vain.
>
> It is true that you live in the midst of difficulties and snares, and you need a double guard of watchfulness

and prayer. But since you know both your need of help, and where to look for it, I may say to you as Darius to Daniel. "Thy God whom thou servest continually is able to preserve and deliver you." Daniel, likewise, was a public man, and in critical circumstances; but he trusted in the Lord; was faithful in his deportment, and therefore though he had enemies, they could not prevail against him.[4]

Encouraged by his mentor's admonition, William Wilberforce continued his fight to end the slave trade; a fight that would last another eleven years. Many more defeats would come, each time prompting William's likely return to Newton's words: "Though you have not, as yet, fully succeeded in your persevering endeavors to abolish the slave trade, the business is still in process."

Wilberforce's task was to call for compassion and justice from an empire that had been callously indifferent to the plight of fellow human beings. Many resented his "self-righteous" accusations against an economic system that enabled their comfortable lifestyles. His was no short-term assignment with a quick win. It required long, determined commitment and the ability to heed the apostle Paul's admonition, "Let us not grow weary while doing good" (Galatians 6:9).

By 1796 Wilberforce had grown weary. But the grace of

persistence shored up his ailing body and tortured spirit, giving him the strength he needed to see another day. On February 23, 1807—twenty years after he had originally taken up the cause—the House of Commons rose to its feet in tribute to William Wilberforce. Cheering the weeping champion of abolition, they proceeded to vote by an overwhelming majority (283 to 16) to abolish the slave trade throughout the British Empire.

A few months later, John Newton, the man who had encouraged Wilberforce to enter and continue the battle, died. But not before seeing the fulfillment of his prophetic admonition of William: "Though he had enemies, they could not prevail against him." And not without seeing his young friend live out the lyrics he had penned many years before.

PERSISTENT GRACE
Lasting redemption often demands persistent dedication.

> *He who has mercy on the poor,*
> *happy is he.*
>
> PROVERBS 14:21

GENEROUS GRACE

As he approached the main building, William Wilberforce shook his head at the stark contrast. Leaving his carriage near St. George's Church moments earlier, he had been inspired by the cathedral's grand architecture and heavenward spires. Few man-made structures could match its declaration of the glory of an almighty God. The structure he entered now, on the other hand, shouted the heartache of a wretched mankind.

Marshalsea was one of the three prominent debtor's prisons in London where those who could not pay their debts were sent. An oblong building partitioned into what Charles Dickens would later describe as "squalid houses standing back to back so that there were no back rooms; environed by a narrow paved yard, hemmed in by high walls duly spiked at top." The intimidating central unit seemed a cross between factory and sanitarium—fitting for a place housing the worst aspects of each.

Knowing this was an unlikely place for someone with the wealth and stature of William Wilberforce to visit, the warden welcomed his guest with cordial embarrassment. "An honor to meet you, my lord," he said. Hoping to prevent a member of Parliament from taking too much notice of the miserable conditions, he pointed up the stairs as he began his ascent. "Perhaps we could chat in my office?"

"That won't be necessary," interrupted William. "I cannot stay long, so I'll come to the point of my visit."

In relieved curiosity, the warden turned back toward his distinguished visitor. "Your servant, sir."

"I understand a man by the name of Jonathan Wade was placed in your custody last month." Wilberforce spoke with firm determination, careful to conceal the contempt he felt for a man apparently unwilling to improve the lot of those under his care. No wonder so many died in debtor's prison, where such unnecessarily miserable conditions only intensified their despair.

"Yes, he was. A sad situation, my lord. Several little ones and a wife left to fend for themselves."

WILLIAM WILBERFORCE:
Generous Grace

William glanced around before reaching into his coat pocket to retrieve a small sack. Certain his deed would remain anonymous, he handed the bag to the warden. "I believe you will find this amount sufficient to fulfill Mr. Wade's obligation. Please pay his creditors and release him tomorrow morning."

The warden clutched the money and looked up from his hand. "I will, sir. Thank you, sir."

"And here is my card. If you encounter any complications, I will intervene." Clearly, this wasn't the first time Wilberforce had secured a debtor's freedom. "I will be in session tomorrow, but word can reach me if sent to this address."

"I understand."

William headed back toward St. George's where his carriage waited in the evening shadows. Pausing, as if remembering a very important detail, he turned to the warden. "And please, tell no one I was here. Not even Mr. Wade."

"But he will wish to know who secured his release. What shall I tell him?"

With a mischievous grin, Wilberforce eagerly replied. "Tell him the Lord God paid his debt."

*   *   *   *   *

After his "great change," Wilberforce famously dedicated himself to two objectives—the end of the slave trade and the reformation of manners. His long battle for abolition rightfully remains his most celebrated legacy. But the second cause, although it received less fanfare than the first, enabled Wilberforce to activate his evangelical passion in helping another group of disenfranchised people: the poor.

Biographer John Pollock said that "good causes attached themselves to Wilberforce like pins to a magnet." He took seriously scriptural admonitions meant to move a believer's heart and hand toward compassionate generosity.

As a private individual, William had a reputation for giving personal gifts whenever he heard of a need. Quite often he gave the money through an intermediary, allowing himself to remain anonymous. Certainly, he had in mind the Lord's admonition recorded in the book of Matthew: "But when you do a charitable deed, do not let your left hand know what your right hand is doing, that your charitable deed may be in secret" (Matthew 6:3-4).

Wilberforce was also known to visit debtor prisons to secure the release of those with no other means to support their families, reminiscent of Jesus' words, "I was in prison and you came to Me. . . . I say to you, inasmuch as you did it to one of the least of these My brethren, you did it to Me" (Matthew 25:36, 40). As a boy, William witnessed his uncle John Thornton's generosity to those in need, modeling the Christian understanding that those blessed with much should share with the less fortunate. As an adult believer, Wilberforce was accused by some of being too quick with a gift. One friend expressed concern that William had been giving money to a sponger, and that he should be more cautious to avoid being taken advantage of. But it seemed William preferred erring on the side of generosity. By the time he was thirty-eight, one year before marrying Barbara Spooner, financial records indicate Wilberforce had developed a pattern of giving away one quarter of his annual income.

William Wilberforce was highly strategic in his giving. While he gave personal gifts to help alleviate misery when it touched individual lives, he also invested generously in efforts that could attack the root causes of injustice and suffering. His "reformation of manners" included an effort to oppose the kind of callous indifference to the plight of the poor he saw among his peers. In concert with his cousin Henry Thornton, Wilberforce began "the Clapham circle," a group of influential men and women living in Clapham and dedicated to philanthropic social reforms. For more than four decades, the Clapham circle launched and supported programs and societies designed to restore moral decency and care for the disenfranchised. Their strategy, put simply, was to "make goodness fashionable" among the upper class.

Wilberforce supported medical aid for the poor after he

discovered that hospitals were illicitly selling medicines for private profit rather than dispensing them to needy wards. When he learned that charity hospitals in London were discharging poor patients before they had recovered enough to earn a living wage, he founded "Samaritan Societies," through which donors could channel gifts to help continue necessary care.

In 1796 Wilberforce played a key role in forming a new organization called the Society for Bettering the Condition and Increasing the Comforts of the Poor—more commonly known as the "Bettering Society." The brainchild of fellow evangelical Thomas Bernard, the society drove scientific investigation of the problems of poverty along with the circulation of information about methods of relief and ways to improve living conditions. They discouraged indiscriminate charity, emphasizing the importance of reinforcing rather than taking away incentives for the poor to work. "In pauperism as in slavery," they believed, "the degradation of character deprives the individual of half his value."[1]

The list of Wilberforce's philanthropic concerns goes on and on. He helped fund a new Sunday school movement which was designed to educate poor children in the Scriptures. He supported "schools of industry" and programs for the deaf. He paid tutors for young men preparing to become ministers, confident that more clergy would mean more individuals watching over the needs of the poor. He also founded the British and Foreign Bible Society because he believed reading the Scriptures could change others as it had himself.

Throughout his lifetime, William Wilberforce gave to at least seventy different evangelical societies, most dedicated to reforming manners by caring for the poor and reducing those things that contribute to the problem of poverty. In 1821 he wrote a brief summary of his hopes for—and satisfaction in—these efforts.

It pleased God to diffuse a spirit which began to display its love of God and love of man by the formation of societies of a religious and moral nature, which have already contributed in no small degree to bless almost all nations. . . . [T]he blessings of religious light and of moral improvement [have resulted in] the growing attention to the education of our people, with societies and institutions for relieving every species of suffering which vice and misery can ever produce among the human race.[2]

William Wilberforce made goodness fashionable by extending the generous grace he had seen modeled for him many years earlier by John Thornton and that he himself had received.

His charitable efforts became a source of great joy and satisfaction at life's end, a happiness each of us can access today.

He who has mercy on the poor, happy is he. (Proverbs 14:21)

GENEROUS GRACE
Grace is extended through charity.

Always be prepared to give an answer to everyone who asks you to give the reason for the hope that you have.

1 PETER 3:15, NIV

COMPELLING GRACE

A small pendulum swung to and fro, its ticks and tocks filling the otherwise silent room. William glanced up at the clock hanging behind Mr. Cadell's London office desk. Nearly seven minutes had passed since he spoke, an occasional sigh of contemplation while rubbing his youthful-looking chin the only signs of interest in the pages before him.

Wilberforce had expected a more eager reception. Hannah Moore had encouraged William to approach Mr. Cadell after reading William's small tract turned lengthy manuscript. Though young, Thomas Cadell had an excellent reputation in the book publishing field, largely due to lessons he had learned while watching his father publish great works like Edward Gibbon's *The History of the Decline and Fall of the Roman Empire.*

Nothing could be worse than watching someone who made his living with books read his first attempt—especially when his disinterest appeared to be growing.

Two hundred and thirty-four clock ticks later, Mr. Cadell placed the pages across his desk in front of William while removing his reading spectacles. Mustering a semblance of enthusiasm, Thomas broke the silence.

"So you began working on this project four years ago?" It was the kind of question publishers ask when they have no specific compliments to offer.

"That's right," William replied. "I began crafting a tract to give to friends interested in my religious convictions. As you can see, it became a bit more than that in the writing."

"Four hundred pages, Mr. Wilberforce, can hardly be described as 'a bit more.' And with the price of paper these days, lengthy books mean heavy risk."

The book had been a labor of passion for William, and he found it difficult to cut anything out. He had lived and worked among so many who embraced a generic religious morality while missing the heart of true Christianity, including his own parents. He knew that real Christianity included some unpopular notions, like sin and repentance. Real Christianity should motivate the upper and middle classes to care for—rather than exploit—the poor and enslaved. A thorough understanding of such a message could hardly be expressed in a tract-length publication.

"I must be honest with you, Mr. Wilberforce," Thomas began as William braced himself for disappointment. "This book is of a religious nature. And while I personally have nothing against your brand of Christianity, I must consider the business realities."

The "business realities" included the fact that Mr. Wilberforce's brand of Christianity had been labeled "enthusiasm" and was considered very unpopular among the educated class.

"How shall I say this?" Cadell continued. "Mr. Wilberforce, those who buy books tend to shy away from religious works. I fear there would be little market."

"I see," William said as he retrieved his manuscript from the desk. "Then I will not take up any more of your time. Why should you publish a book those I hope to influence will not read? Thank you for your time, Mr. Cadell."

As William turned to leave, Thomas began to rub his chin ponderously, as if assembling pieces together in his mind. William's use of the word "influence" had sparked an idea.

"One moment please, Mr. Wilberforce." Cadell suddenly seemed sincerely interested. "As I understand your reputation, you do have a track record of advancing unpopular causes."

"Yes. Thank you. But what has that to do with this?"

"Well sir," Cadell replied, "since your name will be prominently displayed on the book, I believe it might just be worth the risk of printing five hundred copies."

William thought for a moment, optimism overtaking the disappointment of so small a quantity. "Well," he replied, "I suppose five hundred copies would be better than none."

"Indeed it would, sir. I will assign an editor immediately. I've been in the publishing business a long time. But you never know, this book might just surprise me."

"We can hope, Mr. Cadell. We can certainly hope."

✳   ✳   ✳   ✳   ✳

In early 1797 Thomas Cadell printed five hundred copies of a book by William Wilberforce. It carried the cumbersome title *A Practical View of the Prevailing Religious System of Professed Christians, in the Higher and Middle Classes in this Country, Contrasted with Real Christianity*. By the time the year ended, he had gone back to press five times and had sold more than 7,500 copies. The book went on to become a best seller by the standards of the day. *A Practical View* remained in print well into the next century in England and America and was published in five foreign languages.

Historians have compared it to *Mere Christianity* by C. S. Lewis. Like Lewis in the twentieth century, Wilberforce presented his generation with a compelling defense of real Christianity, reaching readers who associated orthodox belief with a lack of sophistication or education. And while Wilberforce may have had no formal theological credentials, none considered him either unsophisticated or uneducated. The author's beloved mentor, John Newton, exclaimed of the manuscript: "Such a book, by such a man, and at such a time!"[1]

The "time" included pervasive disrespect for the emerging evangelical movement labeled "enthusiasm" or "Methodism." Some attacked *A Practical View* as "a very fanatical book." Norwich minister Joseph Kinghorn described early reactions: "He will be called undoubtedly a Methodist, probably a Madman but I think he speaks the words of truth and soberness."[2]

English society embraced what Wilberforce called "mere morality" while giving the particular and essential truths of Christianity little thought. His characterizations could not have been more blunt, beginning with his criticism of parents. "They would blush," he says, "to think [their child] inadequate in any branch of knowledge or any skill pertaining to his station in life. He cultivates these skills with becoming diligence. But he is left to collect his religion as he may. The study of Christianity has formed no part of his education."[3]

Wilberforce goes on to paint an unflattering picture of the average "professed Christian" in his age. "They rarely mention Christianity, and even then only in cold formality. Their standard of right and wrong is not the standard of the Gospel." In fact, he says, "the Bible lies on a shelf unopened. And they would be wholly ignorant of its contents, except for what they hear occasionally in church. . . . Is it not undeniable that with the Bible in our houses, we are ignorant of its contents? In a great measure, the bulk of the Christian world knows so little, and mistakes so greatly, the foundational principles of the religion which it professes!"[4]

As a result of such ignorance, a prevailing attitude that one should elevate sincerity above substance emerged. "Let a man's opinion and conduct be what they may, provided he be sincerely convinced that they are right,"[5] was the cry of the day. Wilberforce disagreed, offering examples of those throughout history who committed "the greatest crimes with a sincere conviction of the integrity of their conduct."[6] Sincere belief, according to Wilberforce, was not enough. It is not *whether* one believes that matters, but *what* one believes.

And what one believes must include a proper understanding of human nature. We are not, as many assumed, naturally pure. We are rather prone to vice, making it easy to sin due to our disinclination to virtue.[7]

Wilberforce's picture of a thoughtful Christianity also included the hope of redemption through Christ's sacrifice on the cross. "Ultimately Christianity restores the whole man, complete in all his functions, to the true ends of his being."[8] And part of those true ends includes behavior befitting one made in the image of God.

Perhaps the most important theme Wilberforce explored was the mistaken notion that one's religion should occupy a limited sphere, impotent to influence one's life beyond the pew. "They assign to religion a plot of land . . . in which it has merely a qualified jurisdiction."[9] Such compartmentalization "assumes the greatest part of human actions are indifferent to religion."[10] The result? A society filled with professing Christians who turn a deaf ear to the cries of human misery among the oppressed and enslaved.

Wilberforce offered readers something very different from the Christianity of polite British society, which biographer John Pollock described as a "blend of a little piety with a little moralizing [that] offered nothing to a man whose inward eye had seen his corruption in the blinding light of the glory of the Lord."[11] In sharp contrast, Wilberforce understood the gospel as "light from darkness, as release from prison, as deliverance from captivity, as life from death."[12]

Wilberforce also confronted the perception that orthodox Christianity was only for the uneducated—reminding readers that Christianity had been embraced, "and that not blindly and implicitly, but upon full inquiry and deep consideration" by such great minds as Francis Bacon, John Milton, John Locke, and Isaac Newton.[13]

A Practical View had an enormous influence among professing Christians of its time, helping to reverse a national trend toward viewing those who took religion seriously as feeble-minded. Wilberforce commended his faith by showing it as intellectually rigorous, emotionally engaging, and practically relevant.

If ever a man modeled the admonition found in I Peter 3:15, it was William Wilberforce. He indeed followed the advice of Peter, to "give an answer to everyone who asks you to give the reason for the hope that you have. But do this with gentleness and respect."

"Such a book, by such a man, and at such a time!" Indeed.

COMPELLING GRACE
Properly understood, Christianity is a most
compelling religion.

Afterthoughts

I, too, have fond memories associated with the hymn "Amazing Grace." If I close my eyes and hum the melody, I can see myself, just sixteen or seventeen years old, sitting cross-legged on the floor of a crowded living room, singing with the gathered faithful until the walls and ceiling shake. I can revisit rallies in parking lots, concerts in gymnasiums, and marches for Christ down Hollywood Boulevard. I can go back to the Jesus Movement of the late 1960s and relive the excitement of tasting God's amazing grace for the very first time.

But for all the poignancy of these personal reminiscences, there's something else of which I'm keenly aware. Having encountered John Newton and William Wilberforce, I realize that I can never approach "Amazing Grace" in quite the same way again. Now that I've come to know the sailor who composed the hymn and the politician whose life was redirected under his wise and patient guidance, I will always hear echoes of *their* experiences of grace in this profound and simple song. Every time I sing it, I will in some sense be thinking of them: of their humility, their perseverance, their tireless devotion to the practical implications of the gospel story. I suppose my rambling verse-by-verse reflections will run something like this:

Amazing grace! How sweet the sound
That saved a wretch like me!
I once was lost, but now am found,
Was blind, but now I see.

When I remember Newton and Wilberforce, I will recall that "amazing grace" is something more than a theological concept in an ancient creed or a beautiful lyric in a beloved song. I will picture grace as a living and active force, a dynamic power with the potential to change lives and turn the world upside down. I will celebrate the grace that seeks the lost and saves the wretch, that gives sight to the blind and life to the dead. I will remind myself that everything I am and everything I have, I owe to the miracle of God's amazing grace. *This*, as I see it, is the central message that sings through every verse of the song and every episode of the lives of John Newton and William Wilberforce.

'Twas grace that taught my heart to fear,
And grace my fears relieved;
How precious did that grace appear
The hour I first believed!

When I ponder the sweet hour in which *I* first met Jesus Christ, I will remember that John Piper speaks of William Wilberforce's conversion as "a great story of the providence of God pursuing a person through seemingly casual choices."[1] I will smile, thinking that the same can be said of Newton, provided we replace the phrase "seemingly casual choices" with "deliberate rebellion and reckless folly." Most important, I will marvel at the realization that this same providence has been pursuing *me* and making its influence felt in *my* life since long before I had the sense to recognize it or call it by its rightful name. How precious indeed is the miracle of relentlessly seeking grace!

> *Through many dangers, toils, and snares*
> *I have already come;*
> *'Tis grace has brought me safe thus far,*
> *And grace will lead me home.*

In one way or another, the life of faith is a struggle for each and every one of us. It's a long road beset with many dangers, toils, and snares. But the task, the goal, and the final homecoming are always one and the same; and the burden is light because we share the journey with those who came before and those who follow after. This, too, is a lesson I will bear in mind whenever I hear the words of "Amazing Grace." For John Newton and William Wilberforce did not fight the good fight alone. The mercy they received and the successes they achieved were all part of a larger plan. Their role was to reap the harvest that the apostle Paul planted when he wrote,

"There is neither Jew nor Greek, there is neither slave nor free, there is neither male nor female; for you are all one in Christ Jesus" (Galatians 3:28). They were following a path that was blazed in the wilderness when Jesus looked at the crowds and said, "Love your neighbor as yourself" (Matthew 22:39). And it was *grace* that led them home.

> *The Lord has promised good to me,*
> *His word my hope secures;*
> *He will my shield and portion be,*
> *As long as life endures.*

From now on when I sing "Amazing Grace" I will be thinking of Newton and Wilberforce and their unwavering confidence, not merely in the justness of their cause, but in the faithfulness of the God who called them to it. I will remember that it was their belief in the *goodness* of the Lord and the reliability of His promises that enabled them to press forward in the face of almost unbelievable tribulations and adversities. Their perseverance and determination to stick to the job, not only until the work was finished but "as long as life endures," were not simply the distinguishing character traits of two unusually gifted men. Instead, this remarkable tenacity flowed directly from a firm conviction that, come what may, "grace would get the upper hand."[2] How could it be otherwise when they lived in the settled assurance that the everlasting Father was their strength and shield (Psalm 28:7)? How could they doubt it when *He* had pledged Himself to be their portion and inheritance forever (Psalm 73:26)?

> *Yes, when this flesh and heart shall fail,*
> *And mortal life shall cease,*
> *I shall possess, within the veil,*
> *A life of joy and peace.*

And yet at last there came an end to all their labor and strife. This, too, is an aspect of God's amazing grace. For in a world like ours, where nothing is accomplished without pain and travail, where "the whole creation groans" under the effects of sin and the Fall (Romans 8:22-23), it is a mercy at length to lay our temporal toils and troubles aside. It is a blessing to finish the race and reach the end of the weary way—to follow in the footsteps of David the king, who, "after he had served his own generation by the will of God, fell asleep." (Acts 13:36). It is a gift of incomparable worth to know that beyond this veil of mortal flesh lies an eternity of joy and peace, a life of unending fulfillment, satisfaction, and repose in the presence of Him who has gone ahead of us to our Father's house. Surely this is what John Newton had in mind when, just a month before his death, he told a young friend,

It is a great thing to die; and when flesh and heart fail, to have God for the strength of our heart, and our portion forever: I know whom I have believed, and he is able to keep that which I have committed unto him against that day. Henceforth there is laid up for me a crown of righteousness, which the Lord, the righteous Judge, shall give me at that day.[3]

Wilberforce lived and died in the same expectation. As Lord Macaulay, composer of his epitaph, observed:

He died not unnoticed or forgotten by his country; the peers and commons of England, with the Lord Chancellor and the Speaker at their head, carried him to his fitting place among the mighty dead around, here to repose; till, through the merits of JESUS CHRIST, his only Redeemer and Savior, (whom, in his life and in his writings he had desired to glorify) he shall rise in the Resurrection of the just.[4]

This, then, is the triumphant chord I will hear ringing in my head every time I come to the fifth verse of John Newton's timeless hymn. I won't be able to sing these four lines without picturing Newton and Wilberforce at the gate of heaven, dropping their burdens at the Savior's feet. Whenever I hear the words *"a life of joy and peace,"* I will imagine them standing there, lifting their eyes to the everlasting hills, basking in the accolades of the Master to whom they dedicated all their efforts. I will hear His voice as He beckons to them from the door: "Well done, good and faithful servant[s]; . . . Enter into the joy of your lord" (Matthew 25:21).

Amazing grace! How sweet the sound! I've always found it so. But it will be all the sweeter to me now that I've walked a mile with John Newton, the former servant of slaves, and William Wilberforce, the tireless and unassuming liberator of the oppressed. Having traveled with them for this short time, I will forever after sing their song in a new and different way. And I will strive to live in the hope that echoes through the sixth and final verse of Newton's hymn:

> *The earth shall soon dissolve like snow,*
> *The sun forbear to shine;*
> *But God, who called me here below,*
> *Will be for ever mine.* [5]

Jim Ware

Endnotes

Maternal Grace

[1] John Newton, introduction by Bruce Hindmarsh, *The Life and Spirituality of John Newton* (Vancouver, BC: Regent College Publishing, 1998), 17.

[2] Ibid.

[3] Ibid., 18.

[4] Quoted in "A Faith Grows in Brooklyn," by Carolyn Drake. *National Geographic*, February 2006.

[5] Newton, Hindmarsh, *The Life and Spirituality of John Newton*, 18.

Warning Grace

[1] Newton, Hindmarsh, *The Life and Spirituality of John Newton*, 24–25.

[2] Ibid., 27.

[3] A. W. Tozer, *The Pursuit of God* (Camp Hill, Penn.: Christian Publications, Inc., 1982, 1993), 69.

[4] Francis Schaeffer, *He Is There and He Is Not Silent* (Wheaton, Ill.: Tyndale House Publishers, 1972), 100.

[5] Newton, Hindmarsh, *The Life and Spirituality of John Newton*, 27.

[6] John Newton, "On Dreaming," *Olney Hymns*, #98.

[7] John Newton, *Letters of John Newton* (Edinburgh: Banner of Truth Trust, 1960), 81.

Restraining Grace

[1] Newton, Hindmarsh, *The Life and Spirituality of John Newton*, 31.

[2] Ibid., 33.

[3] Ibid., 31.

[4] Ibid., 33.

[5] Ibid., 23.

[6] Dante, *Paradiso*, Canto XXXIII, 145.

[7] Quoted in *Out of the Depths* (the *Authentic Narrative* of John Newton revised and updated for today's readers), ed. Dennis R. Hillman (Grand Rapids: Kregel Publications, 2003), 136.

Afflicting Grace

[1] Newton, Hindmarsh, *The Life and Spirituality of John Newton*, 41.

[2] Ibid., 34.

[3] Steve Turner, *Amazing Grace: The Story of America's Most Beloved Song* (New York: HarperCollins Publishers, 2002), 28.

[4] From Newton's epitaph, self-composed, which is inscribed on a marble plaque that hangs in the church of St. Mary Woolnoth, London. See Newton, Hillman, *Out of the Depths*, 158.

[5] Turner, *Amazing Grace*, 29.

[6] Newton, Hindmarsh, *The Life and Spirituality of John Newton*, 36.

[7] Ibid., 35.

[8] Ibid., 42–43.

Preserving Grace

[1] Newton, Hindmarsh, *The Life and Spirituality of John Newton*, 46.

Endnotes

2 Ibid., 42–43.

3 Ibid., 50.

4 Ibid., 51.

5 Newton, *Letters of John Newton*, Letter XVIII, 110.

Illuminating Grace

1 Newton, Hindmarsh, *The Life and Spirituality of John Newton*, 56.

2 Thomas à Kempis, *The Imitation of Christ* (New York: Book-of-the-Month Club/Ave Maria Press, 1989), 30.

3 Newton, Hindmarsh, *The Life and Spirituality of John Newton*, 62.

Delaying Grace

1 Newton, *Letters of John Newton*, 133.

2 Newton, Hindmarsh, *The Life and Spirituality of John Newton*, 75.

3 Newton, *Letters of John Newton*, 187.

Growing Grace

1 Newton, *Letters of John Newton*, 13–28.

2 Turner, *Amazing Grace: The Story of America's Most Beloved Song*, 61.

3 Ibid., 50.

4 Ibid., 49.

5 Hillman, Newton. *Out of the Depths*, 103; and Turner, *Amazing Grace: The Story of America's Most Beloved Story*, 100.

6 Newton, *Letters of John Newton*, 25.

7 Ibid., 86.

8 Newton, Hindmarsh, *The Life and Spirituality of John Newton*, 9.

We know that Newton particularly disliked the doctrine of "instantaneous and entire sanctification" that became popular at this time among some of the followers of John Wesley. See John Piper, *The Roots of Endurance* (Wheaton, Ill.: Crossway Books, 2002), 66, note 63.

Long-Suffering Grace

[1] Richard Cecil, *Memoirs of the Rev. John Newton*; cited in John Piper, *The Roots of Endurance*, 56.

[2] Ibid.

[3] Cecil, *The Life of John Newton*, 155.

[4] Turner, *Amazing Grace: The Story of America's Most Beloved Song*, 87–88.

[5] This fifth verse is not well known today, having been excluded from most modern hymnals.

[6] Cecil in Piper, *The Roots of Endurance*, 57.

[7] Cecil, *The Life of John Newton*, 156.

Sufficient Grace

[1] Taken from the 1662 Anglican *Book of Common Prayer* used at that time. See http://justus.anglican.org/resources/bcp/england.htm, accessed August 31, 2006.

Intervening Grace

[1] Kevin Belmonte, *Hero for Humanity* (Colorado Springs: NavPress, 2002), 33.

Endnotes

[2] Ibid., 31.

[3] Ibid., 35.

[4] Ibid., 34.

Gifting Grace

[1] Belmonte, *Hero for Humanity*, 24.

[2] Oliver Warner, *William Wilberforce* (London: B. T. Batsford LTD., 1962), 25.

[3] Ibid.

[4] Ibid., 26.

[5] Ibid., 25.

[6] Belmonte, *Hero for Humanity*, 51.

[7] Ibid., 53.

Changing Grace

[1] Belmonte, *Hero for Humanity*, 80.

[2] Philip Doddridge, *On the Rise and Progress of Religion in the Soul* (New York: The American Tract Society, 1745), chapter 1.

[3] Belmonte, *Hero for Humanity*, 79.

[4] Ibid., 80.

[5] Ibid., 82.

[6] Ibid., 84.

Calling Grace

[1] Belmonte, *Hero for Humanity*, 88.

[2] Ibid., 89.

[3] Ibid., 90.

[4] Ibid.

[5] Ibid., 136–137.

[6] Warner, *William Wilberforce*, 40.

Disturbing Grace

[1] Brycchan Carey, *British Abolitionists*, www.brycchancarey.com, accessed June 15, 2006.

Persistent Grace

[1] Belmonte, *Hero for Humanity*, 132.

[2] Ibid., 133.

[3] Ibid.

[4] Ibid., 136–137.

Generous Grace

[1] John Pollock, *Wilberforce* (Batavia, Ill.: Lion Publishing Corporation, 1977), 141.

[2] Belmonte, *Hero for Humanity*, 174.

Compelling Grace

[1] William Wilberforce, *Real Christianity* (Portland: Multnomah Press, 1982), xii.

[2] Pollock, *Wilberforce*, 153.

[3] Wilberforce, *Real Christianity*, 2.

[4] Pollock, *Wilberforce*, 3–5.

[5] Ibid., 5.

Endnotes

[6] Ibid., 6.

[7] Ibid., 10.

[8] Ibid., 29.

[9] Ibid., 52.

[10] Ibid., 53.

[11] Ibid., 146.

[12] Wilberforce, *Real Christianity*, 4.

[13] Belmonte, *Hero for Humanity*, 228.

Afterthoughts

[1] John Piper, *The Roots of Endurance*, 124.

[2] Turner, *Amazing Grace: The Story of America's Most Beloved Song*, 87.

[3] Cecil, *The Life of John Newton*, 214–215.

[4] From Wilberforce's epitaph, composed by Lord Macaulay; cited in David J. Vaughan, *Statesman and Saint* (Nashville: Highland Books/Cumberland House Publishing, 2002), 113–115.

[5] "When we've been there ten thousand years/Bright shining as the sun/We've no less days to sing God's praise/Than when we'd first begun." These lines, though much beloved by many singers of "Amazing Grace," were not written by John Newton. They first appeared in Harriet Beecher Stowe's influential antislavery novel, *Uncle Tom's Cabin*, and were formally inserted into the text of "Amazing Grace" by the hymn writer and publisher Edwin Othello Excell for the 1889 edition of R. A. Torrey's *World Renowned Hymns*. See Steve Turner, *Amazing Grace: The Story of America's Most Beloved Song*, 137–143.

Bibliography

John Newton

Bruce, Michael, ed. *William Cowper (Everyman's Poetry Series)*. London: J. M. Dent, 1999.

Cecil, Richard. *The Life of John Newton*. Grand Rapids: Baker Book House, 1978.

Hillman, Dennis R., and John Newton. *Out of the Depths*. Grand Rapids: Kregel Publications, 2003.

Hindmarsh, Bruce, and John Newton. *The Life and Spirituality of John Newton*. Vancouver: Regent College Publishing, 1998.

Newton, John. *Letters of John Newton*. Edinburgh: The Banner of Truth Trust, 1960.

Piper, John. *The Roots of Endurance: Invincible Perseverance in the Lives of John Newton, Charles Simeon, and William Wilberforce*. Wheaton, Ill.: Crossway Books, 2002.

Turner, Steve. *Amazing Grace: The Story of America's Most Beloved Song*. New York: Ecco/HarperCollins Publishers, 2002.

Vaughan, David J. *Statesman and Saint: The Principled Politics of William Wilberforce*. Nashville: Highland Books/Cumberland House Publishing, 2002.

William Wilberforce

Belmonte, Kevin. *Hero for Humanity: A Biography of William Wilberforce*. Colorado Springs: NavPress, 2002.

Carey, Brycchan. *British Abolitionists*. www.brycchancarey.com, 2001.

Doddridge, Philip. *On the Rise and Progress of Religion in the Soul.* New York: The American Tract Society, 1745.

Pollock, John. *Wilberforce.* Batavia, Ill.: Lion Publishing Corporation, 1977.

Warner, Oliver. *William Wilberforce.* London: B. T. Batsford LTD., 1962.

Wilberforce, William. *Real Christianity.* Portland, Ore.: Multnomah Press, 1982.

From best-selling authors
KURT BRUNER and JIM WARE...

Finding God in The Lord of the Rings
Uncover the deep connections between Earth and Middle-earth, and let yourself be newly inspired by this tale of hope, redemption, and faith against all odds.

Finding God in The Hobbit
Jim Ware reveals the latent themes of virtue, salvation, and God's sovereignty that underscore Tolkien's original fantasy of Middle-earth.

Finding God in the Land of Narnia
Discover the deep spiritual themes of redemption and grace found in the popular Chronicles of Narnia series by C. S. Lewis.

Finding God in the Story of Amazing Grace
Bruner and Ware explore God's hand at work in the true stories of William Wilberforce, John Newton, and the end of the British slave trade.

SALTRIVER BOOKS are a bit like saltwater: Buoyant. Sometimes stinging. A mixture of sweet and bitter, just like real life. Intelligent, thoughtful, and finely-crafted—but not pretentious, condescending, or out of reach. They take on real life from a Christian perspective. Look for SaltRiver Books, an imprint of Tyndale House Publishers, everywhere Christian books are sold.

SALTRIVER®

INTELLIGENT. THOUGHT-PROVOKING. AUTHENTIC.
www.saltriverbooks.com

AN AMAZING
AUDIO ADVENTURE

BASED ON THE MAJOR MOTION PICTURE
FROM WALDEN MEDIA

World-class actors, dynamic sound, fully orchestrated score—this exciting adventure on five CDs will draw listeners into the stories of John Newton, William Wilberforce, and Olaudah Equiano, three men instrumental in overthrowing the British slave trade. Their lives converged at one pivotal point in history, stirring the conscience of a nation and changing their world, and ours, forever.

Also includes a free sixth disc with bonus features and behind-the-scenes extras!